WITH US IN THE WILDERNESS

Smyth & Helwys Publishing, Inc.
6316 Peake Road
Macon, Georgia 31210-3960
1-800-747-3016
©2014 by Laura A. Barclay
All rights reserved.

Library of Congress Cataloging-in-Publication Data

With us in the wilderness : finding God's story in our lives / by Laura A. Barclay.
pages cm
ISBN 978-1-57312-721-9 (pbk. : alk. paper)
1. Storytelling--Religious aspects--Christianity.
2. God (Christianity)--Omnipresence.
3. Spiritual healing--Biblical teaching.
4. Theological virtues.
5. Cardinal virtues. I. Title.
BT83.78.B37 2014
241'.4--dc23

2014019009

Disclaimer of Liability: With respect to statements of opinion or fact available in this work of nonfiction, Smyth & Helwys Publishing Inc. nor any of its employees, makes any warranty, express or implied, or assumes any legal liability or responsibility for the accuracy or completeness of any information disclosed, or represents that its use would not infringe privately-owned rights.

Advance Praise for
With Us in the Wilderness

In this series of reminiscences, Laura Barclay explores the nature of faith, justice, and community in ways that engage the reader and invite response. *With Us in the Wilderness* is a valuable resource for shaping spiritual formation in individuals and groups.

—BILL J. LEONARD
James and Marilyn Dunn Professor of Baptist Studies
Professor of Church History
Wake Forest University

This is that rare personal narrative—related with all the immediacy of the events and feelings as Laura lived them, but also with a clear-eyed gift of reflection that invites us into the story. The story we end up sharing with Laura is not primarily her faith and life journey, but a shared journey in which we all have a place. She invites us to rethink how all our stories can be entry points for God's justice, reconciliation, and compassion.

—GAIL R. O'DAY
Dean and Professor of New Testament and Preaching
Wake Forest University School of Divinity

Laura Barclay's stirring spiritual memoir, *With Us in the Wilderness*, is cool spring water to a dry, barren soul. Read it and remember we serve a God who invites us to question, to seek—for it is in our doubting that God reveals himself best.

—KAREN SPEARS ZACHARIAS
Author of *Mother of Rain*

With Us in the Wilderness

Finding God's Story in Our Lives

Laura A. Barclay

*For Ryan, my family, the Huddle,
and all those who have
supported me along the way*

Acknowledgments

Ryan Eller, my amazing spouse, has been enormously supportive of this project. Your love, patience, and encouragement have meant so much to me! My mom, Debra Barclay, offered to review drafts and be as objective as possible. The rest of my family and friends have also continually encouraged me in the process. Keith Gammons at Smyth & Helwys was immediately enthusiastic about this project, as was Jeremy Samples. Thanks for your support and confidence in me. I want to thank the beloved communities of Highland Baptist Church in Louisville, Kentucky; Wake Forest University School of Divinity; and the Cooperative Baptist Fellowship of North Carolina. These three communities have been so encouraging of my calling and partnership that I would not be who I am without them. Thanks to all my colleagues and friends in these organizations! Finally, thanks to the physicians, nurses, and other healthcare professionals who were so gracious, kind, and attentive during a very uncomfortable period in my life. You are truly the hands and feet of Christ daily to so many people.

Contents

Introduction   xi

Part 1: Theological Virtues
1   Faith   3
2   Hope   17
3   Love   33

Part 2: Cardinal Virtues
4   Prudence   53
5   Justice   67
6   Temperance   79
7   Courage   91

Conclusion   105

Introduction

In fall 2012, I started this book during the illness described in chapters 3 and 4 as a way to make sense of and understand what was happening to me. My counselor urged me to create a journal, and in the reflection and writing I realized that God was with me. In reading the Gospel healing stories, I could envision myself, along with the lepers, being touched by the hands of Jesus.

As I experienced a sense of "otherness," I became convinced that we have a hard time seeing that our lives are filled with stories of redemption, similar to those told by our biblical ancestors and the cloud of witnesses that have gone before us. Part of the reason the Bible still resonates with us is that these stories are timeless. We can see ourselves in doubting Thomas, suffering Job, and struggling Ruth. The trouble is that the language is too archaic, or we've read it so many times or not at all. All of these issues can keep us from seeing our stories' similarities to the scriptural narrative.

It is imperative that we learn to tell our stories. In doing so, we can discover new things about God, others, and ourselves. If you learn to tell your spiritual story, you can see God in both the mundane and the magnificent and learn to recognize timeless scriptural parallels. The experience will enable you to shed your feelings of being an outcast and embrace yourself as a fully realized child of God without clinging to guilt or shame.

Sharing our stories with others requires us to be vulnerable. I trust that you will see my vast imperfections as part of my humanness, just like yours. I hope that you will see my strengths as something all of us can achieve. Where you and I struggle, know that we are not alone.

In Part 1, I have organized my stories into chapters based on the theological virtues of faith, hope, and love. Paul describes these virtues in 1 Corinthians 13:13: "And now faith, hope, and love abide, these three; and the greatest of these is love." I believe that he not only lists them but also eloquently describes why they are important:

> If I speak in the tongues of mortals and of angels, but do not have love, I am a noisy gong or a clanging cymbal. And if I have prophetic powers, and understand all mysteries and all knowledge, and if I have all faith, so as to remove mountains, but do not have love, I am nothing. If I give away all my possessions, and if I hand over my body so that I may boast, but do not have love, I gain nothing. (1 Cor 13:1-3)

I have discovered that these three virtues are vital in both my spiritual and secular lives, which I seek daily to merge in living prayer. Although I fall short, as most of us do, I think that seeking to frame my actions and thoughts within these virtues has been a redemptive and uplifting undertaking.

The chapters in Part 2 cover the cardinal virtues that the Catholic Church has long held sacred. Why would a Baptist minister focus on these? I have learned that the brave children of the Protestant Reformation, while taking necessary steps to fight for religious freedom, were guilty of discarding some great traditions along with the bad practices. In the secular world, Plato originally recognized these virtues. They are also found in apocryphal books like the Wisdom of Solomon and 4 Maccabees, and they are touted by St. Thomas Aquinas as virtues that should be synonymous with the church.

While I don't always agree with Aquinas, I like to wrestle with ideas from church history and see if it is possible to reclaim them. In our time, the "ancient future church movement," as many call it, is growing popular. More and more believers are interested in reviving old customs of liturgy and breathing life into them in a progressive context. This method can help us connect to the best of our past while still moving forward and embracing the future of the church in our world.

If even one person reads these stories and begins to write and discuss his or her personal spiritual biography using the reflection questions, I will have fulfilled my mission of empowering others to see God's presence in their lives and to accept their stories as worthy of sharing. Please use this book for personal devotion, in college and adult Christian education classes, for group discussions, and more. May it bring you closer to God and to one another while enriching your spiritual life.

Part One

Theological Virtues

Chapter 1

Faith

Baptism

Like many in my generation, I have found that my journey to faith is complex and multilayered. Though I was born into a Southern Baptist family, my parents doubted some of the more austere elements of the faith, like not allowing women to hold positions of leadership, enduring countless sermons on the fiery pit of hell, and conforming to the authoritarian nature of the pastor and board of deacons who tightly controlled the congregation. This certainly didn't square with their view that "God is love" and their constant assurance that I could grow up to be anything, even the president of the United States.

I asked, both aloud and to myself, "Why can't women lead the offering? Why can't women preach? Why is it that when women speak, it's called 'giving a talk,' and why do they so often criticize what she's wearing?" Church seemed at odds with my parents' ethics and with what I knew of God, and my questioning nature led to many conundrums for my parents, like, *If Santa isn't real, what if Jesus isn't real? How do you know God exists?* I am grateful that they listened patiently, let me ask as many questions as I liked, and helped me talk through these issues.

I can recall several events that shaped my faith. For instance, my mom read *The Adventures of Huckleberry Finn* (first published in the US in 1885) to me when I was eight, and Mark Twain's classic novel has had a profound impact on my moral imagination. Huck is constantly weary of the formality of the church that the widow and his aunt teach him about. After he begins to hide and protect his friend Jim, a slave, Huck feels guilty for disobeying the unjust laws of the state and wrestles with what to do, ultimately choosing self-sacrificing love for Jim, the moral center of the book. "Alright then, I'll *go* to hell," Huck states, mistaking man's law for God's law but still choosing the right and moral decision. This resonated with me, and I talked with my mom about how much I agreed with Huck's choices. I clung to this as I grew older, and now I realize just how formative Mark Twain's theology has been in my life.

A few years after reading *Huckleberry Finn,* I went to church to be baptized, and then I never went back. I remember my parents saying something like, "As soon as you make your profession of faith and get baptized, we don't have to keep attending that church." After all, how can you look your daughter in the eye and tell her that she can be anything she wants to be, even the president, and yet watch her face a completely differently reality in a house of God? Because of the questions I was asking, it was confusing at best and harmful to my confidence and spiritual growth at worst. I think that, on some level, we had all come to see that particular church as being in a different place, both practically and theologically, than we were. In fact, our experience there was so harmful that, despite our intention to join another church as a family, we never did feel comfortable enough to wade in.

Years later, I came to see baptism as the beginning of a commitment, not the end. It marked the start of a faith journey to be taken together in the beloved community of a church. Unfortunately, neither my family nor I felt comfortable in a traditional church setting for a long while afterward due to such a negative environment at that first church. Our experience went against the Baptist tenet of the priesthood of all believers, in which all believers, male and female, are allowed and affirmed to interpret Scripture for themselves and preach the gospel if called. Ultimately, while I view my baptism as an authentic response to God's call and the first step in the long journey of a Christian, I was lucky to leave that church and its negative practices and then to wander in the spiritual wilderness for a while before finding the home to which I was called.

> *Just then a woman who had suffered from hemorrhages for twelve years came up from behind, and touched the edge of his cloak; for she said to herself, "If I can only touch his cloak, I shall be healed." But Jesus turned and saw her, and said, "Take heart, my daughter; your faith has healed you." And from that moment she recovered.*
> *(Matthew 9:20-22)*

Doubt and Questioning

My next encounter in a faith setting was when my parents sacrificed and worked multiple jobs to send me to a private, nondenominational Christian school. While I'm an advocate of public schools, the schools in my county were some of the worst in the state. I still remember the sound of my first grade teacher slamming a paddle down on the desk of a stuttering student struggling to read, threatening to "scare the stammer" out of her.

My high school experience could have been a Christian sitcom. Chapel consisted of contemporary Christian music on rotation and a lot of hands waving in time to the beat of the drum. It was a conservative school, and Bible class was mandatory. One day all the female students were called into a meeting and told that we needed to monitor our skirt lengths because we were in charge of both our purity and the boys' lustful ways. The boys, they explained, couldn't control themselves sexually, and if they got lower grades it was our fault. I hiked my skirt in protest, and one teacher resigned over the blatant sexism. I know that forgiveness is required of Christians, but it remains hard for me to lay aside my anger toward adults who would pile such guilt and shame on young girls for their appearance in a world that already harshly judges women's appearances through magazine covers, TV ads, and peer pressure.

In my sophomore Bible class, I was taught that the downfall of Rome came not from the nation overreaching its territories or being sacked by the Visigoths, but because its people embraced gay lifestyles. Many of us laughed at the absurdity, not to mention our teacher's blatant disregard for historical facts and his picking and choosing of biblical texts. One day a student who was gay but not open about it disappeared and was sent to a camp to "cure" him. This was when I realized I needed to be in a place where I could ask questions without being judged.

After making it through yet another judgmental and condemning faith environment, I wanted to go to a large, public university. I desired to be in an environment where I wouldn't be harangued with lectures on skirt length, could learn new ideas, be allowed to ask questions, and be exposed to a wide array of opinions. I had one last obstacle before such freedom, however. I couldn't graduate from my high school without taking Senior Bible class, where we were warned not to believe what we learned "out in the secular world." Negative views were espoused toward sexuality, delayed marriage, and scientific thought.

High school wasn't all bad, however, because it was a small school that was flexible with leadership opportunities. I did find a wonderful group of friends, and we started a service club; it became mandatory for all students to do two service projects a year. For many, it was their first experience serving others, and it helped them grow in many ways. I learned to manage volunteers, work hard, and make important mistakes in a safe environment.

> *"Truly I tell you: if you have faith no bigger than a mustard seed, you will say to this mountain, 'Move from here to there!' and it will move; nothing will be impossible for you."* (Matthew 17:20)

I entered the University of Louisville terrified but excited about the prospect of all the knowledge I would absorb. Eventually, however, I found a lot of friends who were, like me, "misfits" from the church. They had doubts and questions as well. Some were gay or lesbian. Some were women who had been excluded from certain aspects of the church. Many were looking for a way to mesh science and faith. There is no way to guess how many hours I spent at parties or in study groups discussing faith with people. I never brought it up, but the discussion always seemed to find me.

As a resident assistant (RA), I found that many of my hall mates would confess their doubts to me. Another RA considered ministry, and I talked about faith with him for countless hours. Finally, I knew I couldn't keep running from the question of faith. I knew God was love, but I had no idea if there was a faith community that actually expressed that as a belief.

My only sister, older by nine years, called me shortly after her engagement and told me about a church she had found, Highland Baptist Church in Louisville, Kentucky. She was, like me, wary about church after our experience growing up in the conservative church, but this one was different. It was wonderful, she said, and she wanted me to come check it out. "If you don't like it," she said, "you never have to step foot inside another church." That seemed like a fair deal. I will never forget the experience of timidly walking into yet another church and steeling myself for yet another talk on hell. What I found surprised me, and I felt my dam of sadness begin to crumble. I heard the first sermon in my life on God's love, not God's judgment or wrath. It's a shame that I was twenty years old; that is far too long for anyone to wait to have such an experience.

I wept uncontrollably. It was a salvific moment. I had found a spiritual home—a place to ask my many questions. Maybe I had held on to my faith just long enough to find it. No, that wasn't quite right, I thought. God had held on to me and wouldn't let me go. God came to me through all of those late-night conversations with others at parties, through the doubt, and through the questioning. God came through those conversations with friends and hallmates and fellow RAs. God refused to let me forget that I was loved and that God was love.

Eventually, the pastor, Dr. Joe Phelps, and I talked multiple times. I told him that my friends and I had a problem with a God who excludes others and is fiery and wrathful. To my relief, Pastor Joe said he had a problem with that God, too. That's why he believed in a God who loved us. I remember looking out the window on that beautiful summer day and exhaling, really exhaling, for the first time in a long time. This man—this church—understood me and my frustration. After a few meetings, Joe challenged me to do something about this feeling. Echoing the words of Gandhi, he told me that if I saw something wrong, I had the obligation to be the change I wanted to see. He asked me if I'd thought about applying to Wake Forest University School of Divinity; he felt that I could join with others who wanted to help change the church and see it centered on the message of God's love. After many nights of prayer, paperwork, and reviewing applications, I thought I was ready for divinity school.

Can You Ever Really Master Divinity?

Though I was ready to accept an identity as a Christian and pored excitedly over my textbooks in seminary, I still needed to shrug off my old, unhelpful way of viewing the Bible. I kept asking, "What is the correct theology?" "What is the right interpretation?" I finally realized that these questions are less important than accepting the love of Christ and reading the Bible through that lens. In this way, the degree title "Master of Divinity" is a misnomer. You can never really master divinity; you can only learn to accept the chaos of life and start asking better questions. Everything somehow falls into place when you stop worrying about "being right." I realized that in reading the Bible I was reading ancient and culturally different documents through a modern lens of ambition, correctness, and rightness. I had to follow the Way of Jesus in order to understand the words of Jesus. And that, I believe, is at the heart of our faith—simply following Jesus in love and deed.

It took me a while to realize this. After every class, I would exhaust myself by trying to fit every new fact into my old theology. My fellow first-year students and I finally abandoned this task at the end of our first semester. I remember that a lot of us were celebrating after one final, and I admitted that I wasn't sure how to construct my theology at that time. "I don't know either!" came a chorus of responses. We knew that we had all found a place to examine church history, theology, and biblical studies together, and to find a way to minister to one another and, later, to many others by confiding and learning together in this sacred community. That was enough. Our faith in God—though we believed we understood little about our Creator—and one another would see us through.

Having strong faith isn't having the best theology or the right belief about exactly how the mystery of the Trinity functions. It's accepting that if God is love, expressed in the actions of Jesus, then we are to follow that God according to the two greatest commandments: loving God and loving our neighbors (Matt 22:37-40; Mark 12:28-34; Luke 10:25-28—an idea so central that it appears in three of the Gospels). Faith is exhibited in following the path of Christ, which is why the first Christians were called "followers of the Way" (Acts 22:4). We can have faith the size of a mustard seed (Matt 17:20) and do wonderful things together for the kingdom of God. It's so simple that it can take us a lifetime to figure it out and perfect it, without ever quite hitting the mark. Loving others as we love ourselves is difficult, and it takes constant prayer, humility, and effort. Mustard seeds are small, but the plants grow large and relatively easily in the right climate. We must learn to look for ways to foster our development as "followers of the Way," growing in love for one another and in our thoughts and actions.

When Evangelism Goes Wrong

When I was about twelve, I began to cultivate a meaningful friendship with a boy at summer camp, whom I will call Paul.

We were interested in many of the same activities, like writing and science, and we shared a similar taste in music, movies, and humor. I didn't know anyone else who

> *"Doubt is but another element of faith."* (St. Augustine)

liked Star Wars and alternative rock, so I was thrilled to have someone who made me feel more normal. If I mentioned the name Obi-Wan Kenobi to most kids I knew, they probably would have thought I was a witch. I felt that I could talk with Paul about some aspects of my life that others wouldn't understand, especially some of my more creative pursuits. We exchanged letters, sharing and critiquing stories and song lyrics back and forth. Most of my friends at the time just wanted to play kickball and talk about comic books, baseball cards, and video games. Although I loved trading cards and playing Nintendo, I longed for deeper discussions about a wider variety of topics. Paul was the right friend at the right time to help me develop and channel my creativity.

After camp was over, we spent many hours on the phone together during the midst of his parents' divorce. I wanted to be there for him, as he had been there for me, even though I had no idea what to say or do. I don't think many twelve-year-olds know how to process feelings about divorce, whether inside or adjacent to the situation. It was evident to me that Paul felt powerless, and he coped the same way I still do when I feel that everything around me is out of control: by clinging to logic and blasting rebellious music as a sort of emotional shield.

Over the course of our friendship, I found out that Paul was an atheist. The Southern Baptist church in which I was raised taught us that all those who were not baptized believers would suffer in hell. I was an emotional wreck over this teaching, because I was encountering and befriending an increasing diversity of people who were not religious, had fled the church because of hypocrisy, or were of another religion. My sister's best friend and college roommate was a Muslim. My sister celebrated the end of Ramadan fasts with her, and she helped my sister decorate her Christmas tree. I loved her, knew that she loved God, and felt that there had to be more to this doctrine than met the eye, but I was still afraid because of my church's teachings.

I debated Paul several times over the existence of God—not because I wanted to share my feelings of love for God but mostly because I couldn't bear to think that Paul would suffer in hell. Fear won out over love because of this teaching. It was a fruitless debate because God cannot be proved or disproved. You have to take God's existence on faith and respond to the experience of God in your life. Paul had never experienced God.

If I could turn back time, I would simply listen to him and speak from my experience instead of trying to argue. Eventually, he told me that the parents of other Christian friends wouldn't let him come to dinner when they found out he was an atheist. I was horrified and gave up ever talking to him about religion. Paul needed stability and friendship. "That will never happen with me, Paul," I assured him. "Your friendship means the world to me, and I will never reject you." Those words still sounded hollow to me, knowing that others had abandoned him in the name of the God we all followed. If God is love, then why should we ever exclude others or decline them hospitality?

We lost touch for a while during high school and college, checking in occasionally with one another. I found him again in the Facebook era during my graduate school years in divinity school. I had reflected on our friendship during a spirituality class and came to the belief that while Christians are supposed to share the love of Christ, we are not supposed to berate others with our belief system. Forcing others into the church with the threat of hell seems at odds with Christ's commandments to love and serve others. Christ told us to spread the good news, not to beat others over the head with it until it ruins their opinion of Christ, Christians, and Christianity altogether. This must mean that we approach others as equals and share our life experiences authentically.

I have plenty of friends who are atheists. Some of them even visibly stiffen or shift uncomfortably when they ask what I've been up to and I tell them I'm working on a sermon or a Bible study. That's fine. I'm not going to hide who I am, and I don't expect them to do that either. God has called us to love all our friends and enemies, but—after a lot of prayer and thought—I have come to understand that chasing them and quoting Scripture isn't always the best approach for living out the gospel. It is enough that we are authentically Christian, not separating our life from the life of the church but letting it shine through us.

> "The beginning of wisdom is found in doubting; by doubting we come to the question, and by seeking we may come upon the truth." (Pierre Abelard)

Paul and I still talk occasionally online, and I had a frank discussion with him about five or six years ago. I told him I was sorry about pressuring him to convert to Christianity, especially during an emotional time in his life. He graciously responded that he never felt like I was doing that, merely that I love debating just like he does. He also told me that, unlike some of his friends, he never felt that our friendship was contingent upon his conversion. My eyes welled up with relief, and I knew that he had given me more in our friendship than I ever could have given him.

Reflection Questions

1. What is the first encounter you remember having with religion?

2. Was your first experience with religion positive or negative? How so?

3. If someone were to encounter your faith in the same way you first experienced it, how would you feel?

4. How would you explain baptism and faith to someone?

5. Think about the idea of faith as "following Jesus in love and deed." What does that mean to you?

6. Who encouraged you in your faith? Who or what have you had to overcome?

7. What are some of the biggest obstacles in the story of your faith journey?

8. What do you think of St. Augustine's statement, "Doubt is but another element of faith"?

9. In Matthew 17:20, Jesus states, "Truly I tell you: if you have faith no bigger than a mustard seed, you will say to this mountain, 'Move from here to there!' and it will move; nothing will be impossible for you." What do you think about Jesus' metaphor of faith as a mustard seed?

10. Have you ever approached another person regarding your faith and felt that what you said or did was damaging? What do you think St. Francis of Assisi meant when he said, "Preach the gospel often, and if necessary, use words"?

Chapter 2

Hope

Glimpses of Hope in China

In summer 2004, between my junior and senior years of college, I set off for six weeks to China and five weeks to Mexico. It was an ambitious travel schedule, but I was not one to pass up an opportunity. The first six weeks we would spend studying politics and culture in China, and the last five in Mexico we would live with a host family and study language and culture at the University of Guanajuato. These two very different experiences were challenging and ultimately transformed my spiritual life.

I arrived in Kunming, China, by way of Hong Kong, with a dozen or so fellow political science majors from the University of Louisville. The altitude sickness and culture shock were evident on our first days, as we sipped Coke to calm our loopy heads while we tried not to stare at children squatting to pee in the streets. The people were very nice, but even their body language was entirely different from ours. Communication was nearly impossible, and I felt like I had been dropped into another universe.

I also got sick early on—probably from the differences in diet and bacteria—and I became frustrated at being sick in a foreign country. My professor told me that I shouldn't go to the doctor there because I might end up dead. This region had one of the highest rates of HIV in the world, and the hospital reused needles. While I complained on the phone to my mother, I could hear clicks and other voices on the line, and all of the students' phones mysteriously stopped working for the next few days. The Communist Party emissary assigned to us feigned ignorance, but he began keeping a sharper eye on us. It was clear that we were being watched and monitored.

I say this not to make it sound like I was suddenly transported into an espionage thriller but to lead up to a lesson learned. I was a twenty-year-old spoiled American, used to well-run hospitals and the freedom to complain. Now, I had to stop taking all of those privileges for granted.

When I recovered, I accompanied my classmates to visit some truly dreamlike landscapes, including Buddhist monasteries in the mountains towering high above the local villages. We were paired with Chinese students at the University of Kunming who majored in English. Other than our instructors and the Communist guide, those were the only people with whom we could interact. The student assigned to me had a father who worked for the Communist Party. I asked her if she was Buddhist, and she replied that she and her mother were, but that her father couldn't be until he retired because Communists had to be atheists.

"Doesn't that bother your father?" I asked. "Not having the freedom to practice religion?"

"Not really," she said. "It's better than in America where you have to register with a religion to run for office."

I laughed. That was the first of many interesting "facts" that I learned the Chinese government taught in their schools about America.

One day, a government representative came to talk with us about religion. He said that people had freedom of religion in China, as long as that religion was registered and recognized by China.

"What if it's not a registered religion?" we asked.

"Then it's not a religion," he stated. As good American political science students, we argued that point with him until he became angry and left.

As we journeyed closer to Tibet, we saw Buddhist monks walking through the streets in smaller but beautiful towns like Dali and Lijiang. I couldn't help thinking about the Tibetan monks and how their claims for liberty threatened the careful system of control the government had in place around the country. Certain Internet sites were banned. As the Fourth of July approached, the more difficult it was to access United States websites and our e-mail. Our Communist guide didn't like it when we left the dorm in the evenings in Kunming. "Wouldn't it be better if they were forced to stay on campus so we could keep an eye on them—for their safety, of course?" he asked our professors. I wondered what made him so worried. It's not like a dozen or so college kids who couldn't even speak Chinese would cause much of a fuss. Under the terms of our visa, we weren't allowed to hand out religious or anti-government materials. Our bags were searched as a preventative measure.

For those of you who remember the 1989 demonstrations, it will not surprise you that the oddest and most disconcerting event occurred in Tiananmen Square. Tiananmen Square is the heart of Beijing. It is where the Forbidden Palace is located, as well as Mao Zedong's tomb, and many government buildings that you can walk through if you put plastic bags over your shoes to keep the carpet gleaming red. The Chinese and the Russians, we learned, have a bit of a competition in who can preserve their leader the longest. Russia has a record with Lenin, and Mao wasn't looking so great.

At the popular tourist spot, the Mausoleum of Mao Zedong, mourners lined up to purchase flowers to toss at the glass box containing the body of Chairman Mao; the flowers would be gathered up promptly by government workers and resold in a brilliant revenue venture. As I quietly observed this, a guard with a machine gun forced me out of line and pointed the gun at my face. *So this is how it ends,* I thought. *A gunshot wound to the face in Tiananmen Square. Will I be on the evening news?* One of our professors stepped between us and asked what was wrong. The guard screamed and pointed at my feet. I shrugged in a gesture of confusion, frozen to the ground and staring down the barrel of his gun. He finally pulled a sticky note out of his pocket with three words mentioning items of clothing. One said simply "flip-flop." Flip-flops were offensive? I looked at the dozens of other people in line wearing them and pointed. "Why am I different?" I asked. He shouted something indiscernible, and one of my professors switched shoes with me and got out of line. This appeased the guard, but he continued to stand uneasily close to me the rest of my time in line, though he kept the gun out of my face. To this day, I have no clue why the guard was so close to executing me.

To see Mao's body, you have to look sad and demure and keep walking without taking pictures. Older women were weeping and stopping and had to be thrown out. This is when I realized that in a nationalistic country where the state is in control and religion is highly regulated, people will worship state figures in lieu of God. The people had put their hope in the state because the state demanded it of them. The state wanted to be the answer to everything. Mao was their God, but they were mourning because all they had were their memories of him in office and a fairly well preserved body. I learned a lot that day, and I'm glad for the experience even though it was terrifying.

I remember feeling overwhelmed by sights of poverty. There were people in the streets with missing limbs and with tumors the size of volleyballs. Children hovered outside restaurants, and if you bought them food, a crowd of more children would form, almost taking you over in a wave of hungry, malnourished eyes. It took a long time before these eyes disappeared from my dreams.

I had wonderful times in China mixed with moments of feeling like an alien and moments of anger and confusion. As a consequence, I try to keep in mind how foreigners must feel in the United States. For I was once "an alien in a strange land" (Exod 22:21; 23:9; Deut 23:7; Lev 19:34), and I shouldn't forget how that felt.

The people appreciated any gesture of kindness. For instance, many mothers asked me to hold their children and take pictures because they hadn't met an American before. That level of trust with a stranger was heartening. Admittedly, some thought I was Britney Spears and would grab my blond hair and pull me into a picture, but they did this, too, out of excitement. The calm moments and serenity at the Buddhist monasteries were a delightful break from the bustling streets of crowded cities. Getting lost in the Forbidden Palace was an amazing and beautiful experience. The conversations and reflections on faith and culture were incredible both with my classmates and the Chinese students with whom we were paired. Being in a country so different from my own shook me to the core and caused me to ask, *What things about my faith and culture do I find valuable? What things can I not live without?*

Inbreaking of God's Kingdom in Mexico

I had about three days to recover from my trip to China before heading off to Mexico to stay with my host family.

Lourdes, my host mother, was wonderful. She didn't speak any English, but she helped me with my Spanish. After I told her about my recent trip to China, she shared with me her experience of traveling to the United States, where her daughter now lives. She said that no signs were in Spanish and that no one would stop and help her when she asked. Lourdes wished that Americans were kinder and friendlier to travelers because the ones who came to live with her were so nice. She couldn't figure out why this was.

My eyes were wet with tears as I listened to her story and heard her desperate wish for hospitality. I promised that I would try to help travelers and immigrants when I returned.

> *"Therefore my heart is glad and my tongue rejoices; moreover, my flesh shall dwell in hope."* (Acts 2:26)

Everything seems perfect in Guanajuato. It is a relatively small Catholic town, and everyone seems to look out for each other. The American students living abroad formed a close community, and I met another student from my university, Travis, who became a dear friend. We spend many nights at the local pub discussing the culture and came to realize that faith was central to this community. The church was the physical and spiritual heart. The people, generous and kind, all had figures of Jesus or Mary hanging from their rearview mirrors instead of fuzzy dice (not that there's anything wrong with that, fuzzy dice lovers!). The people lived their faith.

I had a personal experience with this one day when I fell ill. I went to the doctor with sharp stomach pains. The doctor found that I still had my umbilical cord behind my navel and that it was infected and causing pain. This revelation horrified me because I didn't even know it was possible. He gave me an antibiotic but advised rest and surgical removal when I returned to the States (the US doctors scoffed at his advice for three more years until they realized the Mexican doctor was right). I was bleeding out of my navel, a fact that terrified my host family and me. After I got to my home away from home and explained the situation to Lourdes, I stumbled to my room, closed the door, lay down on the bed, and cried, both because of the pain and also for the isolation I felt. Hundreds of miles away from my family, I was alone and in need of an operation in a country where I was still learning the language.

But what did Lourdes do? She knocked softly on the door, brought her baby granddaughter to me while I lay on my bed, and placed the child on my chest to hold. She said that nothing comforts like the sweetness of a baby. Would you put your grandchild in the arms of a relative stranger staying in your house and suffering from a bizarre ailment? I will never forget what she did. Her motherly hospitality made me melt. I knew I was safe in her house. She was like a second mother. And my mother will always be thankful to her too! Bless you, Lourdes.

As I processed both trips, I realized that the ethics taught by a lived faith in the Mexican community had an impact. Those people were visible followers of the Way. They loved God and their neighbors more than I had seen in any community in the world, including the United States. Later, in divinity school, I experienced this level of engaged faith in only a few very intentional churches. While I tend to view my time in Mexico and my time in China as two opposite ends of the spectrum, they were both vital in my faith formation and my decision to listen to God's calling for me to attend divinity school. China had awakened me to my Western privilege. I didn't know what it was like to see that level of poverty, to experience a lack of freedom of religion and speech, to do without things I had taken for granted my whole life. And my experiences in both Mexico and China drove home for me the vast difference in where those two cultures put their hope: the state versus God. The people of Guanajuato embodied a lived faith in God that made their community a much more preferable place for a visitor to live and be accepted. From these trips, I keep asking myself, *What would a visitor say about my community, and where we put our hope?*

The Call

Not long after these travels, a future contained in the realm of politics seemed limiting to me. The political issues facing the nations I visited were dire—from human rights to immigration, food insecurity to economics, freedom of speech to law enforcement. I knew that politicians could affect the lives of people in every nation, but somehow politics didn't seem like the right path for me anymore. After a disappointing Senate internship during the Iraqi War that left me disillusioned and jaded about the role of government, I no longer believed that most politicians ran for office based on a moral imperative. I was losing hope. How could I help to change the world if the system I was training to be a part of was morally bankrupt? Maybe I had lost my naïve perception of politics, but I started to put my maturing sense of hope in God and began to feel an undeniable pull toward divinity school.

Everything had started to feel wrong—my job, my classes, my day-to-day life. It wasn't that I was doing something wrong. It was that I was in denial, and something was missing. After my conversations with Pastor Joe, I was aware of greater questions and problems that I couldn't address through politics. Those needed my attention now and could no longer be neglected. For me to deny them was to deny part of myself that had awakened through my conversations with Pastor Joe and others, as well as through my prayers. I needed to put my hope in something higher, more substantial, and more connected with my experiences and those "misfits" (myself included) who couldn't stop asking the tough questions about the church and never quite felt like they belonged there.

I vividly remember the night I couldn't avoid it any longer. I was sweating, and my hands were clammy. It was fall break of my senior year in college, and I was at home for the weekend. My parents had fallen asleep on the couch while we were watching a movie. I tiptoed away slowly to avoid waking them and pulled the letter out of my bag again. It was from a friend who had already left for seminary. I had written him and told him of my recent thoughts about proceeding with religious studies. He had written back a letter of encouragement, saying that he had seen potential and a light within me that needed to shine, reminiscent of that old hymn, "This Little Light of Mine." I had only to let it shine.

I prayed about the letter and knew what I needed to do. Losing hope in many politicians did not mean that I had no purpose. I was learning that God laughs at the best-laid plans. I was afraid of formally saying to my parents that I didn't want a future in politics, because that would make it real. It would mean that I was altering my course. My life would take a different path than we had all thought.

I steeled myself and gently woke my mother. "I have something to tell you. You know I've been thinking a lot about my faith and my time in China and Mexico. It made me think about the difference that freedom of religion can make in a society. It made me think a lot about hope and where the people I saw got their hope from. I don't really have hope in a future solely in politics. I have a lot to sort out, and I feel I'm being called to seminary to think about those questions in a different way." At least, that is *roughly* what I remember saying. It was likely far more panicky and less organized, with a lot more squeaking and a lot less coherency.

My mother asked several thoughtful questions to see if this was a passing phase, to see what I thought I would do for a career, to see where I was interested in attending graduate school, and to see if I was comfortable making a low salary (not an easy thing for a parent to contemplate when she has come from a humble background). She was supportive, and I felt relieved to have stated my desire openly and for it not to sound crazy. "I know I told you I wanted a career in politics," I said, "but I think God has something different in mind."

About eight years later, as an ordained minister working for the Cooperative Baptist Fellowship of North Carolina, I received a message on LinkedIn (a social network for professionals) from a student who had experienced the same kind of calling crisis. He had spent four years studying finance and excelling at internships on Wall Street. Recent readings of the Bible, especially the story of the rich man who was not willing to give up all his wealth (Mark 10), had spurred his own clammy-handed nights. Now he needed someone to confirm that he, too, wasn't crazy, and that God really was leading him down a different path. This conversation was deeply rewarding for me because it allowed me to examine my own calling story and to hear in his anxieties my own from eight years before. It also gave me hope that God speaks to us in mysterious ways—not always at times that are convenient for us but always at times that are the best for our souls, our development, and our communities.

Awkward Stage

Perhaps nothing screams feeling "alone in the wilderness" like going through puberty. There are few photos of me from my preteen years. Those that I haven't thrown away are stored deep in my parents' house with the threat of serious consequences if revealed. I have terrible, early morning close-ups of their sleepy faces on long-ago Christmas mornings to share if they show my pictures to another living soul.

Why all the secrecy? Well, when I was ten, I had unarguably the worst haircut of my life. The stylist was instructed to cut a few inches off my long, blond ringlets, and somehow I ended up with a bowl cut. I tried not to weep openly in her chair. I was thin and gangly, and now I looked exactly like a boy. I also badly needed braces, which wasn't financially possible for my family for another few years. My extreme lack of beauty only made me want it more. I saw models pout from magazine covers, and I was convinced that if I pouted, I could cover my crooked teeth and look like a model. In reality, I just looked like an awkward kid in a bad mood.

> "And may God, who is the ground of hope, fill you with all joy and peace as you lead the life of faith until, by the power of the Holy Spirit, you overflow with hope." (Romans 15:13)

This is one reason that all the photos of me from that age were terrible and grumpy-looking. I never told my parents why I wouldn't smile, so they prodded me endlessly to grin. This, of course, only annoyed me more.

If I could talk to my ten- to thirteen-year-old self, I would tell her a few things that I could probably still learn from today.

1. You will grow into your own skin. You won't be gangly with a bowl cut forever. You'll grow up and look like an adult, but that has its challenges, too. Be a kid while you can, and try to enjoy it.

2. God loves you. You feel like you are alone in your awkwardness, but you aren't. God is there in this mess with us. God came to us as a child and experienced growing up. God knows the struggles associated with coming into adulthood. Don't be ashamed to pray about it.

3. Please don't mimic fashion models. I'm sure some of them are lovely people, but they shouldn't be your role models. Try to ignore magazine covers as much as possible. I know it's hard in our culture, but they are just trying to get you to feel bad about yourself so that you'll buy their product. Women are better than that.

4. Finally, have hope. You will have the wonderful privilege of a great education. This will be one of the things you prize most in life. Learning in the classroom and learning by listening to others' experiences every day will be a passion for you. You'll draw hope from this, and you'll realize that all of us are together on this chaotic journey through life. You, precious child, are never alone.

It's hard to look back and love ourselves at the most awkward and seemingly unlovable stages, but try. I'm still not there yet, but I'm working on it. Write yourself a letter to the version of you when you were least proud of yourself. Look at yourself through God's loving eyes, and share a message of hope. What would you say to yourself? What would you say to others who are in a similar place? How can we provide hope to those in difficult places who are having a hard time loving themselves? Let's work hard to bring the kingdom of God to those who need the message of hope!

Reflection Questions

1. What experiences have given you hope?

2. Have you traveled anywhere that gave you a different perspective on faith or culture?

3. What privileges have you taken for granted?

4. Have you ever felt like God was trying to talk to you through another person or in a particular experience?

5. Have you ever felt like a misfit? Why and how did that experience change you?

6. Acts 2:26 reads, "Therefore my heart is glad and my tongue rejoices; moreover, my flesh shall dwell in hope." What do you think this verse means? How can your flesh dwell in hope?

7. Have you ever seen someone—a visitor or foreigner—struggling in our culture? How did you help (or how might you have helped)?

8. If someone visited your community—your town, your church, your home—how do you think they would feel about what gives you hope?

9. When have you felt the most awkward, out of place, or unlovable? What would God say to you in that moment?

10. Do you still harbor shame or guilt about a certain time in your life? How can God's message of hope help you to shed those feelings?

Chapter 3

Love

Divinity School and School of Hard Knocks

One of the best and most meaningful times of my life was spent attending Wake Forest University School of Divinity. It was difficult and academically rigorous, but I loved the challenge and felt blessed by how much I was learning. Many of my questions were answered, though most only led to more questions. Most important, I found many others like me who had difficult experiences in church but wanted to serve God. I met dear friends—like Erin, Sara, and Jessica—with whom I could grapple with theological issues and study late into the night. They always seemed to be there when I had procrastinated too much, worked myself into the ground, and needed to blow off steam, or if one of us was facing an existential crisis.

I also met my husband, Ryan, at divinity school. Ryan happened to grow up just forty-five minutes from my hometown and shared some of the same friends; oddly, we had not met before Wake Forest. I had carefully crafted criteria for dating: (1) Never date a University of Kentucky fan (Louisville Cardinals forever!). (2) Never date a boy who has been in a fraternity (some never grow out of the frat house mentality). (3) Never date a guy whose only Xbox games are NCAA Football and NCAA Basketball (Why not just watch ESPN?). (4) Never date a guy who can't cook (I refuse to cook all the meals). (5) Never date a coworker (that is, to put it delicately, muddying the waters).

Right away, Ryan broke rule 1, along with every rule after that, without me managing to care much. He was wearing a UK shirt when I met him, and I was wearing a University of Louisville shirt. At first I thought this meant I was destined to hate him. I was ready for this guy to get a comeuppance, but then he invited me to a "talent show" that night, where he did ridiculous back-up dancing for a rap act, wearing a giant clock around his neck and a visor that said "Hattitude." Anyone willing to make an idiot of himself for a laugh is on the fast track to being my friend. From there we started creating opportunities to be together, like Hebrew study groups with friends where we drank coffee and got to know each other and never cracked a book.

Pretty soon, we were inseparable. Ryan broke down many barriers I had made that were actually working against my faith. I had decided not to marry—a youthful declaration brought on by a more-than-healthy generational skepticism about marriage and a neurotic desire to focus solely on my career for the rest of my life. I'm not saying that marriage is for everyone, but work should not be your whole life. I was a long way from finding balance, but Ryan's presence made me question decisions I had made earlier without really thinking them through.

He also shared stories about his life through a lens of faith that I was still struggling to find. Ryan had the confidence to see God in his life story and to help me find my voice, so long muffled by difficult church experiences. He encouraged me when I wrote papers and told me he had no doubt that I could preach when I entered the class I most feared: homiletics (the art of preaching). That semester, there were about seventeen women and three men in the class. My preaching professor, Dr. Veronice Miles, walked in, saw the gender difference, and said, "Oh Lord, this is going to be a challenge." As a woman preacher, she knew that getting seventeen women to feel confident preaching was a tall order, but she achieved it well.

With the support of Ryan, my friends, and my professors, I pursued ordination. On the day the ordination council was to meet to question my call, I took a nap in my room several hours before I was expected to arrive at the church. I thought that my two flatmates were gone. Suddenly, there was a loud knock at the door. I opened it to find several police officers on the porch and several police cars on the lawn.

"Can I help you?" I asked.

"We have a report of an attempted suicide," the officer responded. I struggled to comprehend. Was this a sick joke? Maybe they had the wrong address.

"No," I responded. "I'm the only one here." And then it hit me. My best friend, Erin, and I lived together in her house, but she had taken on another tenant (whom I'll call Gina), who was going through a difficult time. Gina kept erratic hours, took Adderall to help her study, and suffered from eating disorders, among other things. We struggled to find ways to empower her to get counseling, but nothing

> *"Teacher, which commandment in the law is the greatest?" He said to him, "You shall love the Lord your God with all your heart, and with all your soul, and with all your mind. This is the greatest and first commandment. And a second is like it: You shall love your neighbor as yourself. On these two commandments hang all the law and the prophets."*
> *(Matthew 22:36-40)*

seemed to work, and she did not seem interested in our friendship. What if it all had become too much for her to deal with?

"Hold on a second!" I shouted to the police officer over my shoulder as I ran to open her door. My brain struggled to take in the scene. Gina's body was sprawled on the floor. There were some towels under her, and her wrist was cut. Pill bottles littered the dresser, and her computer was on the floor in front of her.

"In here!" I screamed, and the police and paramedics ran in to treat her. One officer asked me to come outside and answer some basic questions.

"How did you know she was trying to kill herself?" I asked the officer.

"She called her mother to say good-bye."

Another officer came out to tell me that Gina was alive and they were stabilizing her for transport to the emergency room. She apparently had Googled how to kill herself with the pills she had on hand. I watched as they brought her, seemingly unconscious, out on a stretcher. The police told me her mother was arriving the next day.

I called Ryan, Erin, and the church to cancel my ordination council. I cried because I couldn't get the image of Gina's limp body out of my head. She could have died while I slept peacefully next door.

We went to the hospital, and eventually they let me in to see her. Gina was upset and in denial. "I didn't try to kill myself. I was just experimenting. Everyone Googles how to kill themselves. Don't tell me you haven't."

"No, Gina, I haven't. You've been through a lot, and I hope that soon you can begin to talk about what happened. It doesn't have to be with me, but you can talk to me if you feel comfortable. Erin and I are worried about you. We care about you!"

"Stop worrying. I'm a terrible roommate. I know that. I wouldn't want to live with me. I'm not your responsibility!"

We tried get the doctor to keep her for psychiatric evaluation, but the doctor didn't think it was necessary.

"She tried to kill herself!" I exclaimed.

"She says she wasn't serious about it," the doctor responded.

"Well, a lot of people attempt it before they go through with it. I need some time to figure out how to deal with this situation before she comes back home with us."

"We will keep her overnight and then release her when her mother gets here tomorrow."

I'd like to say that things got better, and that this experience drew us closer and we formed a friendship. Instead, after a week in a hotel room with her mother, Gina moved back in with us. She tolerated me knocking on her door to check on her if she was too quiet for too long, and she let us help her make a plan to talk to her professors about the work she had missed. Eventually, though, Gina dropped out of school and moved back home, and we never talked after that.

I rescheduled my ordination council and was ordained. Everything happened in rapid succession after that: I married, graduated, started a new job, and moved in with my husband in the same month. I started having chest pains due to the stress of going through these events so close together; the pains were later diagnosed as anxiety symptoms. About one in five people in America struggles with anxiety, and many of the ministers I know struggle with anxiety or depression. I haven't yet discovered if ministry triggers these conditions or if persons with these conditions are attracted to ministry, but it is probably both. Chances are that you or a close loved one struggles with anxiety or depression, and you are not alone.

Gina truly did not believe that she was lovable. Many of us wanted to befriend her and get to know her, but she put up defenses because she once had confided in someone who had then hurt her. As I started to struggle with stress, I felt lucky to have friends who listened and who pointed me toward a doctor. I was lucky that I hadn't faced so many negative experiences that I'd build up an impenetrable emotional wall . . . maybe just a moat or two.

Because of Gina, I try to keep my eyes open regarding my own self-care, as well being aware of those around me who might be struggling with issues that seem overwhelming. God loves us all, even if we cannot feel it or see it. People love us and value us, even if we trick ourselves into believing that we are not loveable. That is why God's greatest commandment, to love God and our neighbor as ourselves, is such an important foundation of our faith. We have to believe that God loves each one of us so that we are all equally precious before God. Next, we must love ourselves before we love others. This means we must practice adequate self-care mentally, physically, and spiritually. Only then are we equipped to love others in the way we have learned to love ourselves.

The Outsider

I recently went through a prolonged illness that involved lots of doctors and lab tests. My abdomen ached, and my insides seemed to clinch uncontrollably. I felt helpless, stressed, and angry that I was having to take sick days surrounded by heating pads and missing out on being at the office. At first, my doctor didn't want me to travel. Then, when my condition worsened, she asked me to take time off and submit to lab tests. While I initially bristled, I knew it was wise to get to the bottom of my problem so I could move on with my life. I felt more lab rat than human, and my reaction, as a recovering perfectionist, is to retreat and hide when I feel less than my best. During this illness, I began to shun friends and sometimes family in order to wait it out until I "got better." I didn't want to be a bother or a drag on anyone. I even felt timid going to the local park to walk the track.

One day when surrounded by local teens during their track practice, my stomach flopped and I felt extremely nauseated after walking just a few laps. My doctor had warned me that the medication we were trying might cause such a side effect. I instantly felt like I was back in high school. What would happen if I threw up in front of these teens after merely walking? I talked myself through it. So what? It's not like no one running track has seen that. I ran track in high school and saw people barf constantly during practice. Still, I lacked all temerity in action even though those around me assured me I was fine.

> *"There is nothing love cannot face; there is no limit to its faith, its hope, its endurance. Love will never come to an end."*
> *(1 Corinthians 13:7-8)*

And, because I'm very stubborn, I still needed more assurances that it was all right to leave the house when ill. Christmas Eve night, my husband practically had to drag me to midnight Mass at an Episcopalian church near Lexington, Kentucky. I was still recovering, and midnight church seemed low on my priority list. I sat down hesitantly in the pew, feeling nauseated. The nausea got worse after the incense ball was brought out in the processional. I rolled my eyes and looked at the ceiling. *Seriously, God? I can't deal with your heavy perfume right now!*

Instantly, I was examining the program, wondering how long until the service was over. The first thirty minutes seemed to crawl, and I could focus only on my physical discomfort and pain. What if I got sick in this beautiful, sparkling, opulent church? Then, I began to notice that directly in front of me, a single mother sat with her daughter and autistic son, who was getting frustrated sitting still and began to wail and hit himself on the head. *I feel you, kid,* I thought. Several times during the service, she took him to the back and calmed him before returning to the pew, looking embarrassed. *Oh, no,* I thought. *I hope she doesn't think we mind! She doesn't need to remove him.* Just as I thought that, the mother leaned forward and apologized to the man sitting in the pew in front of her. He turned with a puzzled look in his eye and said to her, "Don't you be sorry. This is exactly where you are supposed to be." He spoke these words to the mother, but they cut through my soul.

As we stood for Communion and sang "Away in a Manger" about our lowly born Savior, that man's words fell upon me in waves of grace. We all wanted to comfort the mother, but I realized that, if I became sick in the church, they would feel the same way for me. We all belonged there—the single mother; the autistic son; the sickly, recovering perfectionist minister; and the lowly born, impoverished baby Jesus who would one day grow up to be our Savior.

All of us struggle with a desire to belong, and the only thing that can soothe it is to love one another in community. This means not hiding our struggles but sharing the burden so that it is easier to bear. During my illness, the therapist asked, "What if there is no 'getting through it'? What if it's about living in the moment?" That reality of not speeding through life's storms but "learning to dance in the rain," according to a saying on my doctor's wall, is much easier when you open yourself up to loving and being loved, and truly believing that you are worthy of love in God's eyes.

Living Into My Vows

In the middle of my illness, I hated sharing my feelings of vulnerability even with my husband, who may be one of the most gracious and compassionate people I've ever met. The woman he fell in love with was funny, outgoing, fearless, independent, and stubborn. I worried that prolonged talk that showed a different side of me would make him doubt his love for me. This is ridiculous, but it's an accurate reflection of how tired I was of feeling sick and how much it was altering my perception of reality. I would frequently answer that I was fine when I wasn't, and I insisted on doing things for myself that I should have let him do for me.

I told my therapist about this, and she asked me if I took care of Ryan when he got a cold or the flu. I replied affirmatively without hesitation, telling her I even enjoyed making herbal home remedies to ease his suffering. "Then," she replied gently, "don't you think you need to give him the gift of being able to uphold his marriage vows of 'in sickness and in health' as well?" Of course. I realized then that retreating from him and not sharing would make him worry more. I have a weakness of being able to advise others while at the same time being clueless about my own emotions or their ramifications.

After I came home from my counseling session, I talked with Ryan about my reluctance to share. I told him that I hated that he was seeing me sick and withdrawn and unsure of myself. I shared my fears that it would change his feelings for me, and it was one of the hardest and most humbling conversations I've had in my life. Yet it was also one of the most rewarding. He responded with shock. Of course he loved me and wanted to be there for me. He was a little scared, but only because we were waiting to see what the plethora of tests would show. Ryan reassured me that I didn't need to hide from him or to hide how I felt.

Though this was a difficult conversation for me, it reminded me of where our marriage is rooted. We made our vows before God, our family and friends, and the Christian community. Marriage is about love, selflessness, joy, and sacrifice. Those elements are needed from both partners. If times get rough, you are invited to be the presence of Christ to your spouse. In being there for one another, I have been reminded many times about God's love and commitment to us as we are committed to each other. Even though some stages of marriage may be difficult, there is an assurance in our vows like God's covenant with Abraham and Noah. We know that we can rely on one another, and that we are empowered by the other's love. I hope to impart this image when I am asked to do premarital counseling and preside over weddings, and it is my joy as a spouse to know it intimately.

Téa Sophia

I now understand what people mean when they say your heart grows larger when children come into your life. The birth of my niece Téa brought our family closer, and it was also endearing to see a little person do some of the same things I did as a child (my sister, Jeri, has jokingly called her "Little Laura"). From screaming rock songs to calling the candy Smarties "Farties" to singing "Happy Birthday" on her kid piano in a theatrical way that would endear her to Elton John, Téa is a constant laugh factory.

But Téa is also a physical reminder of my priorities. When I visited my parents' house for Thanksgiving in 2010, Téa was two years old, and I was eager to see what she said about each holiday. She was becoming more aware and more fascinated by her surroundings, especially by the lights and sounds of the Christmas season.

As her mother and I explained Thanksgiving and Christmas, Téa understood that one of them was Jesus' birthday. We kept working to distinguish the two and told her that we would start to celebrate Jesus's arrival after Thanksgiving. Thanksgiving Day came, and Téa sat at the table, eating her food and smiling at each of us. She got down from her chair after eating, ran around playing, and gave out hugs. Soon Téa lay on the floor, crossed and raised her legs, clasped her hands, and looked up at the ceiling—an exercise she's done since before she could walk that we've affectionately dubbed "baby yoga." She seems to do this when she's thinking or wants to relax.

Téa looked at Jeri and asked, "Where Jesus? I thought we see him today. He come see me?" After a moment of "awwws" from the family, my sister explained that Jesus was always with her and loved her very much. She looked up at the ceiling, resuming her "baby yoga," and thought for a minute. "He love me?" she asked. "Yes, Jesus loves you very much," my sister replied. After a few more minutes in thought, Téa resumed her playtime with constant commands that Uncle Ryan "be a giant" and chase her. Before the week was out, we had built Téa her first fort and invented games that she played for the first time as if they were magic.

This childlike wonder at the world, with its close by-product of hope, was infectious. The commercial aspects of Christmas annoy me, and I've struggled to stake a claim on the meaningful aspects of the holiday. As Christians, we must do this in order to honor the reason we celebrate. It may be as simple as finding a child who reminds you to look for that star in the East as a sign of hope, rather than to be consumed with the bargains of Black Friday. That child might inspire you to watch for the newborn that will be called Emmanuel, God With Us, who will show us a new Way and let us know that we are truly the beloved of God.

During Christmas 2011, I was sitting with three-year-old Téa and watching a video about Jesus that she had chosen. She was obsessed with figuring out who was good and bad in every story, and, keeping this in mind, I watched as she absorbed the content in the video.

A pleasant little boy started off by explaining that the Jews were poor, hungry, and tired of being treated badly by the Romans. His introduction led into a story where Simon Peter was depicted as being angry at Matthew, also called Levi, the tax collector, who was a Jew working for the Romans (though he would eventually become a disciple).

> *"There are three things that last forever: faith, hope and love; and the greatest of the three is love."*
> *(1 Corinthians 13:13)*

"Peter's bad?" Téa asked.

"No, he's just angry because he wishes Matthew wouldn't work for the Romans. The Romans are hurting the Jews. But Matthew leaves his job, and both he and Peter end up helping Jesus," I replied.

"Oh, okay," she said.

Next up was the story of John the Baptist, looking every bit the part of the rough wilderness type. His stern demeanor convinced Téa that he was bad.

"He's bad," she said, pointing to John in the water.

"No, he's helping people," I told her.

"What's he doing to Jesus?" she asked.

"He's baptizing him. That means he's putting him in the water, and Jesus is saying he will follow God." How do you explain such a complicated thought to a three-year-old?

"He's appetizing him?" she asked. I struggled not to snicker as I imagined John the Baptist shoving mini quiches from a serving tray into Jesus' mouth. I put my arm around her.

At that point, John was pictured in jail at the hands of Herod.

"But he's in jail, so he's bad," Téa pointed out.

"The people in power were bad, and they put him there," I explained.

"Oh, okay," she said, clearly trying to process what it all meant.

More exchanges followed, but she had fewer questions during the stories of the miracles of Jesus, which were told more simply. She asked to watch the video again. After it was over, she looked up at me and said, "God helps us."

How, after my fallible attempts to explain what was going on in terms a tot could understand, did she get that idea from the show? Touched, I hugged her and said, "That's right, and God loves you very much, just like we do."

Later, Téa repeated that truth to her mother and father while explaining to them what we did all day. Her parents beamed, proud that she had learned such a message of love. Somewhere in the mystery of a child's growth and a family's love, I learned that children absorb things we could never dream, and they sometimes get right to the heart of the matter. It's always easier to carry the love of Christ in my heart after being around my niece. It is much easier to understand why Jesus was so protective and empowering of children. "Let the little children come to me," he says in Matthew 19:14.

Perhaps one of the most comical and poignant moments came the day after four-year-old Téa had built her first snowman, reaching a noble one-and-a-half feet tall, and she bounded into the house and declared proudly to us all that his name was Tito.

The next day brought the bright morning sun, which reduced Tito to a pile of mush. I came down from upstairs and found Téa sitting by herself with huge tears falling silently down her face, clutching something close to her chest, and looking out the window at Tito's remains.

"What's wrong?" I asked.

"It's Tito. He went away." She looked up at me with big, sad eyes.

"Well, he will come and play with you the next time it snows. But it's okay to be sad. It's sad when something we care about goes away. What do you have in your hand?"

She showed me a picture of her on a "pirate" ship with her Mommy, Daddy, Nana, and Pa.

"Does remembering a really great moment help when you are sad?"

"Yes. I had fun because I was with family and we sang pirate songs!" Téa looked momentarily upbeat before remembering Tito's demise.

"It's okay to be sad," I assured her. "And we need to enjoy when we are happy and take a picture with our minds so that we can think of it again when we are sad. Building a snowman is one of the best things about winter. Being at the beach on a pirate ship with family is one of the best things about summer. The great thing is that we know those times will come again, and we can create new happy memories."

Téa nodded, gave me a hug, and said she needed to think about it for a while and wanted to be alone. Ten minutes later, she had processed the loss of her buddy and was ready to create a new memory, bounding into the kitchen to help Mommy cook breakfast.

This moment stuck with me as a primer for dealing with grief and loss during the holidays. I thought of it as a trial run and a way to dissect my own feelings about loss on an elementary level. I realized that in teaching a child, you always learn something yourself. In going back to the basics, we can get to the heart of human processes and thoughts on the most visceral level and reexamine our lives through the wonder of a child's eyes.

REFLECTION QUESTIONS

1. Do you or someone you know have feelings of anxiety or depression? If so, how were you/they diagnosed? Have you ever gone to a counselor?

2. Have you ever experienced suicidal thoughts or been close to someone who did? Did you/they ever act on them?

3. When have you felt like an outsider?

4. Have you or a loved one ever experienced a serious illness? How did that make you feel at home, work, among your friends, or in your faith community?

5. Have you ever felt uncomfortable or unloved in a church? What made you feel this way?

6. What are some of the most difficult moments you've had with a spouse, significant other, or family member?

7. When has it been the hardest to be vulnerable with a loved one?

8. If you've had children, what lessons of love have you learned from them? If not, how have the children in your life affected you?

9. Why do you think Jesus was so insistent that we have "faith like a child" (Luke 18:17) and that children should not be kept from him (Mark 10:14)?

10. Jesus said, "You shall love the Lord your God with all your heart, and with all your soul, and with all your mind. This is the greatest and first commandment. And a second is like it: You shall love your neighbor as yourself. On these two commandments hang all the law and the prophets" (Matt 22:37-40). Why are these the two greatest commandments, and how have you experienced them in your life?

Part Two

Cardinal Virtues

Chapter 4

Prudence

The Worst Handwriting in History

The biopsy results were supposed to come in the mail, except the handwriting was smudged beside the blank to the right of "Biopsy." It could have said anything from "OK" to "Yikes." In my optimism, I chose to believe it said "OK," but my husband insisted I leave a message with the nurse to confirm. It was a few days before Christmas, and I never got a return call, which I explained away due to the staff's Christmas vacation travels. I called again after New Year's and still didn't get a response, which annoyed me. Then I called nearly a month after the biopsy and explained to the receptionist, "I realize it's not likely I have cancer, but I need to know and the office form was smudged."

"Oh, my God, you *do* need to know! I will call you back immediately with the results."

One hour bled into two, and then I realized I couldn't concentrate on anything but considering a future against the backdrop of cancer. Were they not calling because office protocol dictated that the doctor must tell me in person, or because everyone in the office was very busy, or because everyone in the office had the attention span of a gnat? I had an appointment about two weeks later and thought, *Oh, God, whatever the answer, please don't let me have to wonder for another two weeks!* I felt isolation even as I imagined the support of family, friends, and coworkers. The lyrics of Amos Lee's "Jesus" playing over my iPhone suddenly stood out in my ears: "Jesus, can you help me now?"

How would I tell people? I imagined the looks on their faces. I pondered the finality of the words, "I have cancer." Like BC and AD, my life would be divided into "before cancer" and "after cancer." Not to mention I'd had relatives who died of cancer; I knew of none who had gotten the diagnosis and survived. While my husband's presence and support meant the world to me, his words, "It's probably not cancer," did nothing for my nerves. "Probably" and "cancer" are two words that don't go well together in a person's brain, even if the word "not" is between them. I needed scientific results.

I had errands near the doctor's office, so I justified that it probably wouldn't be too weird if I went in and asked for the results. I carefully explained why I was there, but the staff seemed bewildered as to why I didn't wait for them to call after leaving messages for a month. The administrative assistant offered to print my test results if I would wait for about fifteen minutes to see the nurse. She handed them to me, and I sank down in a chair in the empty waiting room.

"Has 2 cancers," read the doctor's note scrawled at the bottom of the page of indecipherable lab results. *This is it,* I thought. How would I tell Ryan? How would I tell my parents? My sister? My niece? I imagined the looks on their faces, and I knew that would be what I dreaded the most. I wondered what I would look like bald and if I had a funny-shaped head under all my hair. Maybe shaving it off would be empowering, like all those scenes in movies and TV shows. As these thoughts raced through my head, my body grew numb.

"Laura Barclay," the nurse called. I followed her back as she huddled with me in hushed tones. She described the test in terms I struggled to understand, talking about polyps and how they can be cancerous and noncancerous.

"But mine is cancerous?" I blurted out.

"No," she said, unbelievably.

"But it says on the form, 'Has 2 cancers.'" I pointed to the paper.

She squinted and shook her head. "His handwriting is terrible. It says, 'needs 2 concur.'"

My eyes widened. "Are you sure?"

She nodded and smiled.

"No cancer?" I had suddenly only developed the capacity for short sentences.

"No cancer," she confirmed.

I left the office, and when the cold winter air hit my face as I stepped into the parking lot, it reminded me that I was alive. I stopped and bent down, three choking sobs escaping from my mouth. I was emotionally spent. I went home and muddled through telling Ryan the good news, laughing like a madwoman. Then I sequestered myself on the couch watching sitcoms for three hours and sleeping until I felt like I could join the human race again.

I thought about my aunt and great-grandmother who had died painfully of stomach and colon cancer, respectively, and realized that one day this could be my fate, but I had to live life in the moment, not knowing which breath could be my last. I thought of all those who might have received a different diagnosis that day, reeling from the news and struggling through telling loved ones. I knew I might have spent one of my nine lives, but I needed to learn from it.

Prudence teaches us to discern between courage and recklessness, bravery and stupidity. I could commit to living each day to the fullest without deciding to become the first person to go around the world in a rowboat, especially considering that I have no seafaring skills of which to speak. I renewed my commitment to exercise almost daily and eat more fruits and vegetables, treating my body as a temple. I needed to take care of myself so that I could care for others.

Jesus' greatest commandment is that we "love others as we love ourselves" (Matt 22:39; Mark 12:31). But the stated implication is that we must have begun to love ourselves, to cultivate practices to be kind to our minds, bodies, and spirits. Stated slightly differently, the Dalai Lama, Nobel Peace Prize Winner and Tibetan Buddhist teacher, said, "If you don't love yourself, you cannot love others. You will not be able to love others. If you have no compassion for yourself then you are not able of developing compassion for others." This means getting enough sleep, eating well, giving myself permission to have fun and rest, and learning to say no, which is hard for women and ministers—and certainly for women ministers! I am far from perfect on this, but I've had huge areas of growth because of this negative experience. Through my meditation on prudence, a potentially emotionally crippling experience became a point of growth and actually improved my quality of life.

The Mountain

On my trip to Guanajuato, the personnel from the study-abroad office organized a hike out of the city and up a local mountain. We trudged for about an hour outside of town, the landscape sandy and dotted with cacti, and up a mountain that had a calm waterfall down the side. What started as fun became a little scary as we continued to climb up the ever-steeper wet slope without harnesses.

"Just a bit further," the guides kept calling down to us.

We finally reached the top and had to make it over a crevice near the edge to arrive on the peak. I vaulted through, swinging my legs and steadying myself with my arms. I briefly looked over the steep edge to the valley below, then turned to help the others coming behind me. After assisting five girls, I miscalculated and turned to walk along the edge of the path where everyone else was gathering to rappel down the mountain. Another girl vaulted over the crevice and knocked into me by accident, sending me teetering toward the edge. I saw my death. It would be ugly, and I would hit a lot of cacti on the way to the valley below. I instantly thought, *So this is it. I wish I had done more with my life.* And then I went over. Something halted my fall and pulled me back, dropping me on the plateau path. I looked up and there was Arturo, a classmate who had vaulted over at the last minute, saw my tumble, and grabbed my shirt. I clung to the rocky mountain path and cried "Thank you!" to Arturo. My whole life really had flashed before my eyes, and I knew I wanted so much more.

There was not time to reflect on my near fall, and I would not be allowed to develop a fear of heights. The only safe way down was to rappel several hundred feet to the ground. I gulped air and backed over the side, saying a quick prayer and locking eyes with a study-abroad adviser to give me courage. My friend Travis was on the line next to me, and it was at least nice to back into nothingness with a buddy. Partway down, I let myself fly a bit and screamed in exhilaration. It was fun! I decided to take the positive rappelling experience with me, not the negative one where I nearly fell off the mountain.

Years later, I sat in Buddhism class in divinity school, and my professor led us on a guided meditation. While deep in thought, I saw the mountain in my mind, hundreds of years before I arrived. I saw my near end. I saw myself rappelling and laughing down the side of the mountain. I saw it in present day. The mountain was not the enemy. It merely existed, and my experiences and what I took with them were mine to sort out. I felt gratitude for these experiences as I realized something. The nagging feeling that I wanted more out of life before Arturo caught me had helped guide me to divinity school. I would not be who I am without both the bad and the good. Prudence is associated with wisdom. That does not mean that we never make mistakes; it means that we learn from the mistakes we make. I should be afraid not of the mountain but of failing to learn from my experiences. I should be afraid of leading what Socrates referred to as an "unexamined life."

The Journey Home

Eighty percent of people who are born in Kentucky die in Kentucky, supposedly the highest such percentage of any state. I have no idea if this is a correct statistic. I couldn't find it with cursory Google searches, and I'm not sure it matters. Almost every Kentuckian I've met who lives out of state gets a wistful look in their eyes when they talk about home. When I left for graduate school in 2005, I wasn't sure if I would ever come back. I viewed life as a progression, in that typical American fashion, toward bigger and better. Who knows where life would lead, and I didn't want to make any promises on returning as a twenty-one-year-old. A series of events led me toward the inevitable, however. First, I married a North Carolinian who was raised in Kentucky. Each time we went back to visit family, we looked ever more fondly on our home state. Second, we had family members get sick and die, and we wished we had been there to care for them. Finally, we fell in love with the state all over again by finally doing the things we never really did when we lived there—learned about innovative faith communities, attended horse races, went on part of the bourbon tour, and explored and learned about the culture and history.

We took the time to cherish our roots. I read Wendell Berry's *Jayber Crow* and thought about my grandparents' fierce desire to grow and can all their own vegetables the old-fashioned way. I wanted to be more self-sufficient. These economic times call for it. We saw the state and the people for the beauty they hold, and the vision captured our souls.

We thought and prayed about this pull to return home. Ryan got a job working as an online community organizer, and I started to feel led to give back to the state where I was born. As I pondered this, my heart started to break when I thought about leaving my coworkers and council members at CBF North Carolina. This moderate Baptist denomination had been my home. These folks had loved me, mentored me, empowered me, and embraced my calling. They also had been clear that they wanted me to follow my calling, wherever it led.

The greatest gift, which I didn't understand at the time, was when, several years before, executive coordinator Larry Hovis had related a story to me. Larry told me that his father had owned a mechanic shop in Charlotte. He trained lots of young workers who eventually went elsewhere. Larry asked his dad, "Do you ever get mad that you invest in these people and then they leave?" His father replied, "No. I get the privilege of training the next generation and knowing that they are out there doing good work." Larry told me that if I was ever called to move on, he didn't want me to hold back because we were all like family. "But," he added, "please stay as long as you want! This is the best team we've ever had, and you're a part of it!" His words echoed in my head as I delayed a decision for months. Housing prices were starting to increase, and I knew we were running out of time to make a reasonably priced move.

Ryan and I made the choice a week before the last CBFNC General Assembly. It was difficult going through such a large and stressful event knowing that it would be the last with my coworkers. I didn't want to tell them before; then we'd all be more stressed! When I did tell them a few weeks later, I struggled to fight back tears. I would miss this family away from home. After many hugs and blessings and jokes and some tears, I set out for Kentucky and a new chapter. But I will always keep my years in North Carolina, along with the friends I made and the lessons I learned there, close to my heart.

It's hard to make big, life-changing decisions, especially when you aren't single. You have to take into account the well-being of your spouse or any kids and extended family you might have. There are also budgetary and career concerns. A necessary aspect of prudence is discernment, and that can be key during these times. It's helpful to have a series of discussions with your spouse and think about it over time. Yet, at the end of the day, a large shift will always feel reckless. Even after months of thought, prayer, and consideration, I felt a bit like I decided on a whim to join the circus.

Following God can be like this. If you are open to seeing where your calling and your gifts are leading you, they can take you to the most surprising places. They can even take you home.

Confronting Nightmares

I have a history of terrible dreams. When I was a small child, I would dream that the devil was coming to get me, materializing out of the ground as a glowing, red, shadowlike being who would drag me down to his underworld. This was most likely the confluence of listening to many a dark sermon on hell and an overactive imagination. After several years of constant parental assurances that the devil wasn't coming for me, I graduated to terrifying dreams about school. These involved a lot of the usual: finding oneself nude while walking down the hall, realizing you have to take an exam you didn't know about, or having to repeat grades due to a mistake in the school records. Sprinkled into these typical nightmares was also a breed of night terrors like my childhood devil dreams. Some had *Twilight Zone*-like plots, probably because I liked to stay up late and watch old episodes of that show. Others were inexplicably morose, involving characters from my real life or faceless men in suits.

In college, I had a recurring bout of nightmares that kept me from sleeping for much of my sophomore year. It always started the same. Several faceless men in suits and fedoras would kill a close friend. I would happen upon them killing a friend in the parking lot of my dorm or on campus, and scream for them to stop as they delivered the final blow. Then, I would spend the rest of the dream running from them. Through backyards, interstate car chases, and airport concourses, they followed me relentlessly.

Over and over, I would wake in cold sweats, scrambling, believing I was being chased until I was fully awake. I would lie there and wonder why these dreams wouldn't go away. I prayed about them to no avail. I became frustrated by the lack of response from God. Eventually, I made an appointment with the university counseling department. I felt ashamed to go because I didn't know anyone who was open about seeing a mental health professional. I also didn't know how common or healthy it was to see one on a regular basis. I was far from alone in asking for help, but I was a few years from a level of maturity and knowledge that would have made me comfortable sitting across from a therapist.

The psychiatrist immediately tried to prescribe sleeping pills, which I refused. I was so timid about the appointment that I certainly wasn't comfortable with accepting a medicinal solution at that point. She sighed and said, "All right, well, what if you confronted the men in your dream?"

"What do you mean?"

"You said that they are chasing you. Are they armed?"

"Yes. They usually have guns."

"Okay, then. Before you go to bed, say to yourself over and over that you have a gun and you will face your attacker. It's worth a shot to try to get that message into your subconscious."

I agreed and promised her that if it didn't work, I would return for more assistance and consider taking sleeping pills.

For the next several nights, I envisioned myself with a gun, dressed in superhero clothes, and ready to fight. The first few dreams after my session with the psychiatrist, I would see the faceless men kill my friend, and then I would run toward them to fight. Still waking in sweats, I kept up the routine of envisioning the defeat of these men. Finally, toward the end of the week, I fought the men and shot them. I never had the dream again.

This isn't to say that I don't still have nightmares. As someone who is prone to anxiety, I actually have many of them. But I know that if I get into a rut of horrible, recurring dreams, I have a tool to empower myself and my subconscious against my fear. I learned that maybe God didn't answer my prayer in some mysterious way to vanquish my dreams, but I was pointed in the direction of the counseling office. This solution also empowered me to learn the tools to target my own struggle, which is invaluable in the world of mental health.

Counselors on college campuses often serve as the hands and feet of Christ, helping struggling students deal with living on their own and the challenges that come with growing into an adult. From body image issues and sexual assault to anxiety and depression, these counselors are a vital part of the university support system. If you are a college student in need, consider making an appointment. If you are an adult, there are therapists in your area if you need help. Or, if you know a counselor, thank them for all their difficult work!

Reflection Questions

1. Meditate on a time when you were challenged. What happened? How did you feel?

2. How did you get through this experience? How did you cope?

3. What lessons did you learn?

4. How did your life change? What it a positive or negative change?

5. How did your family, friends, or coworkers support you?

6. How did this experience affect your faith? Did you find it harder or easier to pray, read Scripture, attend church, or talk with others about God?

7. Have you ever had a brush with death? Did it change you?

8. Have you had to overcome any fears? If so, what were they, and how did you work past them?

9. Think of when you had to make a big shift or change in your life. How did you make the decision? How did you feel as you started a new chapter?

10. Has God answered your prayers in ways that were different from what you expected?

Justice

Justice for Hector

One normal Thursday in summer 2010 was unforgettable and life changing. A heated political issue took on a human face for my coworkers and me when one of the pastors in the CBFNC Hispanic Network of churches was arrested. Sheriff's deputies arrested Reverend Hector Villanueva in front of his children at his home on the morning of Thursday, August 19, simply because he had applied to become a citizen. Though he'd had a green card and a Social Security number for decades, he had once served time for trying to cash a bad check when he was homeless in California in the mid-1990s. Because of an inane law in US immigration policy, anyone who isn't a US citizen can be deported if they have been convicted of a felony, regardless of whether they have paid for their crime.

Shortly after his arrest in California, Hector had become a Christian and worked hard to minister with others. He moved to North Carolina, married a US citizen, had four children, and adopted two more, including one with special needs. Hector started churches with the help of Reverend Javier Benitez, CBFNC's Hispanic leader coach, and exhibited love for his neighbors. My coworkers and I wrote character reference letters to encourage the judge to grant a petition for bond, which he did, but the road was still long. Hector awaited trial at home with his family, and my coworkers and I, while trying to mobilize people to advocate for Hector, felt relatively helpless against such a confusing, overwhelming immigration system. Hector's wife, Martha, remained a rock to her children throughout those weeks, and I was amazed by her strength and composure when we spoke.

Friday, September 2, 2011, over a year after Hector's initial arrest, he appeared in court for his deportation hearing. CBFNC staff organized ministers and laity to pack the courtroom in support, and Hector gave compelling testimony about his transformation in serving God through his ministry and his commitment to his wife and children. The judge, moved by his testimony and our support, said that he was convinced of Hector's "rehabilitation" and canceled his deportation. The judge carefully reminded him that he could never be a citizen under current US immigration law, though his wife and children all enjoy that privilege.

Relief and joy washed over Hector and his family, reverberating throughout the CBFNC network. We received countless messages of support and prayer for Hector when the verdict was announced and during the year leading up to the hearing. The fact that Hector is barred from citizenship is a reminder to us that our system is flawed and there is little room for grace. States across our union are faced with these realities every day. Denominations sued the Alabama state government in 2011 for violating the practice of their faith by passing a law indicating that anyone who aids an undocumented immigrant will be arrested. Arizona requires all immigrants to carry and show their papers. In North Carolina, the CBFNC Hispanic Network of Churches is facing a growing crisis. Police officers camp outside their churches, checking the documents of drivers entering for worship.

Many of our Hispanic pastors, who are citizens or legal immigrants, have to drive vanloads of members to church because the police can only check the driver's identification. Our current system is broken, and our immigration quota system has barred many immigrants from ever obtaining citizenship. This means that there is no line for those without documents to get into in order to immigrate legally.

We as Christians are called to respond to our neighbors. In Matthew 25:40, Jesus reminds us, "Truly I tell you, just as you did it to the least of these who are members of my family, you did it to me." Whatever your opinions on the particulars of immigration reform, the gospel is clear in how we should treat the strangers in our midst.

One night after I spoke with Martha, I recognized my level of privilege. In high school and college, I knew friends who were arrested for possession of drugs, driving drunk, and failing subsequent drug tests but who have not served any time. Moreover, they had their crimes expunged from their records. We see celebrities get slaps on the wrist for repeated crimes and misdemeanors. I find it difficult to understand why there is a law stating that non-citizens who serve time for a crime, even though they have paid their dues, can be deported years later when they have clearly been bettering society for years. Those of us who have the privilege to be heard must work with those who are treated poorly until that blessed day when we are all counted as equals in our land, though we are already equal before God.

Lobbying for Our Neighbors

After Hector received the good news of his cancelled deportation, CBFNC was asked to participate in a number of venues to tell our story and to contribute to a solution. One such opportunity came in April 2013, when a representative of the Baptist General Convention of Texas asked us to help with a lobbying effort of a large group of evangelicals who were sharing their story in Washington, DC, to ask for fair and comprehensive immigration reform.

I scrambled to set up a press conference in Winston-Salem to tell local pastors' stories and explain why we wanted immigration reform. Then we challenged elected officials to respond because we were coming to ask them to act in a few weeks in DC. This level of action may make some people uncomfortable. I think many moderate people in the church have seen political action harm churches and cause difficult splits, the most obvious of which was between the Southern Baptist Convention and the Cooperative Baptist Fellowship in the early 1990s. Almost every denomination has a similar story, however, and many are due to a rift between ideologies.

I believe that there is a vast difference between political action for the sake of one's neighbor and partisan favoritism that threatens both the sanctity of the church and the First Amendment. The former follows our Lord and Savior, Jesus Christ, who was accused of a political crime. In Luke 23:2, the assembly who brings Jesus before Pilate states, "We found this man perverting our nation, forbidding us to pay taxes to the emperor, and saying that he himself is the Messiah, a king." Jesus was not simply perceived as someone who was protesting the Roman government; the people didn't believe that he even recognized its authority!

The latter partisan pandering is a dangerous game. When we align ourselves with a political party and equate it with righteousness, we are perverting our faith with an entity that exists to raise money and obtain power. Churches aligning themselves with the state have caused untold suffering throughout history, including crusades, inquisitions, and executions. It is of utmost importance that people of faith be a prophetic witness to our government to remind them of why they were elected, show them who is suffering, and work to empower others to share their stories with people in office. We must avoid being the ones who perpetuate oppression.

I was honored to accompany many CBFNC Hispanic pastors to DC to help them navigate the halls of government. As a privileged white person, I recognized that I could help them get in the door. After that, however, immigrants should be the ones to speak. This issue is their experience alone, and they can speak to the arrests, racial profiling, and suffering in a way that I cannot due to my lack of direct experience. Those with privilege should take care to empower those marginalized by society, not further silence them by speaking for them.

Because of my faith, I believe that history is on the side of the righteous and those who fight for equality and dignity. Those struggling for civil rights may have endured fire hoses and beatings, but they won because their cause was just and rooted in God's command of love. Similarly, I believe that immigration reform is an issue that will be won because of the dedication of immigrants enduring arrests, familial separation, and living in hiding. Churches are also helping by marching alongside immigrants and creating the platform for them to tell their stories. As Martin Luther King, Jr., related, "The arc of the moral universe is long, but it bends towards justice."

"The Love of Money Is the Root of All Kinds of Evil" (1 Tim 6:10)

Recently, two of my family members were laid off by two different corporations because, in both cases, the corporate executives chose making more money over quality of work. For one of these family members, it was the second time this had happened in five years. In all three cases, the layoff was because of money. Paul was right. The love of money is "the root of all kinds of evil." It changes people. It makes them care about things that don't matter—things that no one can take with them when they pass. It makes them forget about the greatest commandment—to love God and others as we love ourselves. The more I shared my family's story, the more I heard the same story echoed from middle managers, paralegals, and even ministers. Dysfunction amid recession, the need for scapegoats, discrimination, and greed were common threads in the stories of how these people were discarded. Instead of valued as precious children of God, each of them was expendable. In a world with a population of over six billion, people are an inexhaustible resource to corporations.

Often, those in power seem to focus on the "love yourself" part of the greatest commandment. Their purpose is all about profits and bottom lines instead of caring for employees and building something for the common good. My family has undoubtedly suffered because of the love of money.

We're all caught up in it. We're all richer than most of the world's people. We're all buying from or working for corporations who feed this system. We live in one of the richest nations in the world. If a family of four in the United States makes $50,000 after taxes, they are in the richest 5.8 percent of the world's population. Their income is more than fourteen times that of a typical person elsewhere in the world. And, if that family donated 10 percent of their income, they would still be in the richest 6.8 percent of the world's population and have thirteen times the income of the typical person. (If you're interested in finding out how wealthy you are by comparison, visit http://www.givingwhatwecan.org and scroll down to "How Rich Am I?")

We often ask, "What would Jesus do?" But it's hard to say what Jesus would actually do today. He didn't really have a job, and he remained firm in his mission until his death in a territory ruled by Rome. The United States is the Ancient

Rome of the modern world. We are considered the world's police, and our president the most powerful leader in the world. What a privilege it is to be a US citizen. But how disturbing that this means we have more in common with the rich Pharisees than with Jesus, who was not a Roman citizen but an impoverished, Arab-looking, troublemaking radical. This is not to say that we haven't had experiences like Jesus had when we felt belittled or nameless in society. But, if we follow his ethic, we know a few things: we are supposed to love God and our neighbors, and we're called to see and care for the poor as if they were Jesus.

How can we do this in a way that hints at justice and works toward righting economic inequalities? We can support businesses that pay living wages and carry fair trade items that provide reasonable compensation for workers. We can recognize that, despite our circumstances in the United States recovering from a massive recession, we are wealthy beyond comparison. We should give thanks and think about what we can do with our combined wealth.

What we do in this world matters. How we treat others matters, and it will leave a legacy to guide younger generations. What example should we model in today's economic climate?

The Trial that Defined a Community

Many of us are beneficiaries of a great struggle that we don't know much about. Most people will never know many of the individual stories of the civil rights movement, women's rights movement, or labor movement. For eight years, I had the privilege of calling Winston-Salem my home. A number of partnerships between black and white clergy exist in this town, mostly due to a controversial trial that was settled before I ever set foot in North Carolina.

Darryl Hunt, a young, African-American male, was arrested in the mid-1980s for raping and murdering Deborah Sykes, a copy editor who worked for the local paper. What local police ignored, however, was that her murder was part of a larger string of attacks and that Hunt had alibis during those other attacks. A completely white jury convicted him on scant evidence. Hunt languished in prison for several decades. When DNA testing became possible in the mid-1990s, Hunt's DNA was tested against that collected at the crime scene. It showed unequivocally that Hunt was innocent, but the judge would not allow the verdict to be overturned. Hunt was confined for ten more years, even though he had already proven his innocence. Over time, ministers mobilized. At this point, the facts in the case showed such a huge miscarriage of justice that clergy of all races were united in trying to bring the true circumstances to light. Relationships were built across color lines, and there was an understanding that a problem for one neighborhood was a problem for everyone.

Eventually, Willard Brown, another convict already in prison in Georgia, confessed to the crime. Hunt sat in prison for a few more months, but he was finally released due to community pressure. Darryl Hunt used the money subsequently awarded to him by the government for wrongful imprisonment to form a nonprofit, The Darryl Hunt Project, that assists those who are jailed for crimes they didn't commit. Unfortunately, his story is indicative of a larger problem in Winston-Salem and the South, with many black men being arrested and imprisoned by all-white juries over very little evidence. Now that clergy from across the community are more vigilant, we can only hope and pray that this type of injustice will become less prevalent over time.

When I arrived in Winston-Salem to attend Wake Forest University School of Divinity, I attended workshops on cross-racial partnerships, and later, at the Cooperative Baptist

Fellowship of North Carolina, I underwent more intensive training on fighting racism. I was able to work on racial reconciliation in churches because of the template provided by Winston-Salem clergy in the wake of the Darryl Hunt case. My husband, Ryan, served as a community organizer in Winston-Salem. He once rode to a meeting with Hunt and noticed that his dashboard was filled with receipts. He asked him why he had so many, and Hunt responded that he wanted frequent timestamps in order to provide an alibi for "when he was arrested again." Notice that he said "when," not "if," feeling that the police would inevitably frame him once more.

In my training and relationships with clergy and lay leaders from other cultures, I discovered that their reality was different from mine. Police checks are still more frequent in black and Hispanic communities, a truth reflected in a recent court case that involved dozens of documents provided by the ACLU against the city of Winston-Salem. Prisons are disproportionately filled with African-American males. Predominantly black schools rank lower on test scores and graduation rates. Blacks have significantly higher rates of unemployment and underemployment in the community.

As I moved back to Kentucky, services to help such communities were being cut. The shining beacon of hope remained the clergy and faith communities who were, and still are, willing to speak truth to power, to learn about the plight of their neighbors, and to commit to acting with them in empowering ways. These clergy are living into the image of justice reflected in 1 John 3:16-17: "We know love by this, that [Jesus] laid down his life for us—and we ought to lay down our lives for one another. How does God's love abide in anyone who has the world's goods and sees a brother or sister in need and yet refuses help?"

I owe a huge thanks to Darryl Hunt, all the clergy and attorneys who helped free him, and the multitude of others whose struggles allow me to live into my calling today. From movements in women's rights to civil rights to religious freedom, I am in awe of the cloud of witnesses who came before me. Can you envision all those who battled for justice so that you could thrive today?

Reflection Questions

1. Has a political issue ever become personal to you?

2. How did you react?

3. Are you friends with someone outside of your economic class? If so, how did this relationship form?

4. Why do you think many people don't have friends outside of their race or economic class?

5. What does God's dream of justice and reconciliation look like for us? How do you live into that?

6. What is the difference between social justice and charity? What did Jesus mean when he said, "The first shall be last and the last shall be first" (Matt 20:16)?

7. What is the difference between partisan politics and political action?

8. Have you or someone you loved ever lost a job? Have you ever fired someone? How did this make you feel?

9. What protections do workers have against joblessness?

10. Make a list of the struggles and people throughout history that allow you to function as a full member of society. Give thanks for their commitment to God's vision of justice.

Temperance

Politics and In-laws

Since I am a person who can be passionate about certain issues, restraining my anger has been a huge struggle for me. My parents love to provoke me by taking opposing views, even when they could not care less about a particular policy, just to see how fast I come up with an argument and then laugh when I lay out my beliefs. It is typical youngest child torture and a game my parents delight in far too much. As a political science major, I come by contentiousness honestly—I was taught to debate!—but it has been a struggle to let it go. It's been easier to do as I get older and watch politics tear our nation apart and divide families.

Whatever your political party, chances are high that you have Republicans, Democrats, and possibly Independents in your family, whether you are aware of their affiliations or not. This is certainly the case among my relatives. When I was home at Easter a few years ago, my husband and I had dinner with my parents, as well as Ryan's father and stepmother. For the first time, our two families ventured into a deep discussion of religion and politics. Let me stress that our religious and political views are many and varied. I shifted nervously in my seat, hoping we wouldn't hit a verbal wall as topics related to immigration, health care, and racism arose.

I kept waiting for the other shoe to fall, but I'm glad I didn't hold my breath.

In the middle of the discussions and negotiations, we kept finding ways to affirm our respect for one another. Perhaps it was the shared underlying belief that we are all made in the image of God. "I don't understand where you're coming from" became "How much can we agree on?" Eventually, we were experimenting in public policy with statements like, "If we were to introduce a bill on immigration, on what topics could we agree to start forming statements?" The conversation ended with laughter and a solid agreement on the need for term limits and for honesty about mistakes, corruption, and greed on both sides of the aisle.

Now, over the course of the last year, we have watched heated ideological differences lead to yelling, spitting, throwing bricks into government offices, growing militia movement numbers, and open-carry rallies that weren't even about gun rights. We've watched some Republicans criticize a Democratic president for negotiating a new START nuclear treaty with Russia, though President Obama used the same negotiation terms that Republican president Reagan used in the 1980s. Conversely, President Bush was never heartily celebrated by many Democrats for his commitment to global AIDS relief or for declaring certain environmentally endangered areas to be protected near the end of his presidency.

If we stop seeing the image of God in our neighbors, regardless of their political party or religion, then we fall into the trap of belittling them or inciting violence against them. Perhaps if both parties could find a way to humanize the other side and figure out what we can agree on, rather than boiling the sum of a person down to a list of issues, we could all sit around a table and laugh like family.

Seeing my family sitting around, joking together and meeting each other in the middle across political lines, renewed my faith in God and in the virtue of self-restraint. I had missed the mark or, rather, sinned when I believed that I could argue someone into agreement. That is another form of bullying. Instead, we should build relationships with one another and learn from each other. Both sides should be willing to be open to change. If neither party is willing to be vulnerable, the relationship is not authentic.

Temperance is about finding balance, restraint, and humility. We can only do that if we first believe that we do not have all the right answers, regardless of our faith, denomination, citizenship, political party, economic class, gender, skin color, language, sexuality, or any other category we can come up with to divide us. Only God has all the answers. We are tasked with loving one another—not with being right and getting others to take our side. Of course, loving people who are very different from us might be harder than arguing with them, but that's the price we pay for deciding to follow Jesus.

Asking for Help

In planning the annual Cooperative Baptist Fellowship of North Carolina General Assembly, two things happen: (1) the CBFNC staff feels sure that this will be the best assembly yet, and (2) in order to cope with the stress of planning the best assembly yet, we fall into unhealthy eating habits, celebrating something called "Random Lard Days." This is when a staff member brings in donuts, bagels, cookies, cupcakes, and other sundry items loaded with sugar and/or dough. Preferably both.

Before one assembly a few years ago, I failed to notice that my other colleagues were delegating some of the work to capable and helpful volunteers who would make their life easier though collaboration. I was going through a time where I overextended myself, raising my hand for everything, and my catch phrase that year was, "I can handle it."

This phrase became my worst enemy as the day of the General Assembly approached. I had continual nightmares. In my dreams, I overslept and missed the assembly. I mixed up schedules, and angry workshop leaders demanded compensation. I tripped over my words in front of the congregation who looked up at me disapprovingly, and then I tripped over the pulpit, crashing into pews and knocking myself out. That's right—in my nightmare, the assembly came to a screeching halt in a pulpit-smashing incident.

It's amazing how our brains play tricks on us when we allow unreasonable fears to creep in. Despite the fact I was surrounded by an amazingly supportive network of staff, ministers, and laity who would never react this way, my subconscious did somersaults in my sleep. I would wake up after a few hours, hands clammy and sweat on my brow, puzzled with myself for my outlandish dreams.

Instead of relying on others, I found myself running audio recorders to workshops, delivering and picking up attendance slips, taking photos, leading a workshop, and putting out fires everywhere. I was my own worst enemy. By the time the thirteen-hour workday was over, I had run roughly five miles in, around, and throughout the church without hardly any rest to shove food in my mouth.

When the event was over, I caught a bad cold. I had been eating poorly, not exercising regularly, and putting too much of the "success" of the event on my own shoulders. This was my fault alone, and I was angry with myself. Next year, I promised, I would build into the process a way to recruit and work with local church volunteers who could take on some of the load.

I consider myself to be a collaborative person, but in crisis mode I want to ease others' anxiety and take everything on myself. This is well meaning, but it is a form of vanity or pride. No one but God can take on everyone's anxieties. Ministers, or anyone in any career who tries to be a perfectionist, will burn out trying to be "saviors." This isn't our job. Our job is to fulfill our calling as children of God who exhibit the love of Christ to one another. We can do this by empowering each other and giving our neighbors tools to solve their own problems, not by doing everything for them. To take on every burden is to distort our purpose, to distort our relationship to others and God, and to give ourselves a recipe for burnout, anxiety, and depression. Judging by the rates of mental illness in our country, this is an epidemic.

Instead, we must embrace humility as an aspect of temperance, which requires collaborative leadership and asking for help. It means that we should admit when we are wrong; it means we aren't the only ones who know how to do something "right." Approaching life as a constant student ready to learn helps us bolster our skills but also keeps us open to better methods and practices.

In subsequent years, I became much better at delegating, asking for help, and being clear about my boundaries. Fewer items slipped through the cracks, I remained more cheerful, I was motivated to exercise more, and I made better decisions regarding food *outside* of work (who can resist an office lard party?).

Every year was a learning process, but my last with CBFNC was my best. I relied on others in a collaborative way, I communicated responsibilities to others clearly, and I had more energy throughout the process. I didn't get sick afterward, and I made a point to continue exercising and eating right. I still struggled with sleep the week of the assembly, but the nightmares I had were even more ridiculous. They caused me to wake up laughing instead of sweating. In one dream, I arrived at the church to find a grizzly bear roaming the halls. I had to call animal control to deal with the situation before people arrived to attend workshops. In another, my coworker Gail and I were frantically coloring a mural of pirates to welcome people to the assembly. Apparently, my supervisor had decided that our theme was being changed to "missional pirates" at the last minute. These dreams, I realized, meant that the staff and myself were completely prepared for the event. The only thing that would throw us off was the unforeseen and absurd, which we couldn't control. I laughed at my dreams and eased into assembly weekend calmer than ever before.

Lessons from the Greatest Generation

While I love my maternal grandparents, I only recently had the opportunity to feel that I have a lot in common with them. My grandparents, Mammaw and Pappaw, have lived all their lives in the same several-mile radius in a little town called Waco, Kentucky. The only time Pappaw left the country was when he was stationed near Hiroshima, Japan. He arrived soon after the nuclear bomb "Little Boy" destroyed the city.

My grandparents still don't own a computer, so it's hard for them to understand my world of blogging, social media, and communications, or to see the scope of the issues I support, like immigration reform.

Likewise, it's hard for me to see their perspective. I've had the privilege of earning scholarships that paid for much of my travel to countries that weren't affected by war. I wasn't raised on a farm as they were, so I never knew how to garden or hunt or fish or can, which are frequent topics at their house. For most of my life, I rarely knew how to begin to cross the generational divide between us.

Thankfully, several things occurred that have brought us closer together. First, I lived with my friend, Erin Goddard, in divinity school. She had both learned from and taught at the Folk School in the mountains of North Carolina. Erin knows how to do so many things that have been lost to my generation, like weaving, spinning, cooking, and fixing just about anything. Seeing her abilities made me want to learn more, and I knew that my grandparents could teach me.

Then, a few years ago, I had a strong desire to begin gardening. Part of this, I'm convinced, is in my blood. It skipped a generation because my mother is not big on digging in the dirt, but I sometimes crave the feel of dirt on my skin and the sense of accomplishment after I've weeded, planted, or mulched. Now that I've moved back to Kentucky, my Pappaw supplies me with tomato plants, and I report any discoloration in leaves, infestation, or lack of growth. He gives me pointers to keep the plants healthy.

My interest in history has connected with Mammaw's desire to see all her pictures and memories recorded. My mother is collecting photos to label and make into a visual family tree. I've asked questions to fill in the blanks and keep the stories preserved for the next generation. I've learned that both sides of my family have lived in the foothills of Appalachia for multiple generations, and I want the children in our family to be proud of their heritage. Mammaw also loves to go antiquing and learn about old furniture, as I do now that I've furnished my Depression-era home with period furniture I've collected from yard sales, websites, and the Habitat Re-Store.

Finally, the recession has caused my generation to be frugal out of necessity. As the market changes, many in Generation Y don't experience job security, and it's wise to learn a variety of skills that can help us cut down on costs and be better stewards of the environment. It's a good idea for us to learn to be self-sufficient, by growing our own food rather than purchasing commodities that have to travel across continents and learning to do the things that our Baby Boomer parents didn't have to know because of their long years of job security through the late twentieth century. It's time to reclaim the wisdom of our elders and no longer depend on technology as our sole means of survival. Learning their skills can bridge divides between our families, bring us closer, and, ultimately, give us a legacy for the next generation. God gave us dominion over the land, and it would be a shame if we forgot our connection to it.

The Joy of Uncomfortable Discussions

A few years ago, I was privileged enough to be one of the hundreds of participants at the Baptist Conference on Sexuality and Covenant, a project sponsored by both the Cooperative Baptist Fellowship and Mercer University. This was in response to numerous issues that partner churches and ministers were dealing with, including cohabitation before marriage, divorce, delayed marriage, widows and widowers living together, and homosexuality.

The conference planners were intentional about having attendees break up into diverse small groups and maintain the same discussion partners throughout the event. After hearing a few speakers, we would go into our small groups and tackle tough topics together. We made a covenant to be honest about our hopes and fears, not to interrupt one another, not to attack anyone's experience, and not to share stories outside of the group without permission. In my group of about a dozen people—black and white, young and old, gay and straight, female and male, conservative and liberal—all shared their stories. I discovered that some issues that could be vitriolic in the public sphere because of antagonistic political talking heads became real, tangible, and worthy of holy listening and discussion. It was heartening to hear people on both sides of various sexual issues share deep personal experiences and come to an understanding of one another's humanity. No side was railroaded or belittled.

I made some deep friendships in that small group, and I interact regularly through Facebook with about five of the twelve participants. It was the most beneficial, useful, and meaningful conference I've ever attended. The structure made participants commit to be vulnerable and discuss tough issues. For instance, I had never even thought about issues regarding elder sexuality. Many people cohabitate after former spouses die but choose not to get married because of the way government benefits are structured or due to complications regarding estate planning. Does this make their relationship less valid?

One thing is certain: churches don't like talking about sex. It makes us uncomfortable right down to our Puritanical roots. It's easy to thrust all our shame and fear about tough topics on others when we are confronted with an issue that makes us feel awkward. However, Scripture warns us repeatedly not to act out of fear and to temper our responses. Jesus reminds us in John 14:27, "Peace I leave with you; my peace I give to you. I do not give to you as the world gives. Do not let your hearts be troubled, and do not let them be afraid." We must approach life with a heart of peace and a desire to triumph over fear.

A kingdom of God response would be to make space to talk about whatever issue is affecting our church or community and participate in healthy, holy listening grounded in humility. Only when we are willing to listen to others without reservation can we truly perceive their struggles and shed our misconceptions. Any other course of action can split churches, cause heartache, hurt families, and, ultimately, disregard Jesus' greatest commandment to love one's neighbor. How can we continually be the presence of Jesus in difficult situations?

REFLECTION QUESTIONS

1. What issues are stumbling blocks in your life? Anger? Vanity? Something else?

2. How has this put a wedge between you and God or others?

3. Have others helped you learn to channel this stumbling block into productive energy?

4. When in your life have you found it the most difficult to achieve balance?

5. Do you work collaboratively? If so, give an example of when this worked best. If not, why? What makes you reluctant about working in groups?

6. What gives you the most anxiety in your job, home life, and/or social life? How do you deal with that anxiety? When has it been the strongest? What has helped you the most?

7. What difficult issues have you or your community experienced? Did you respond out of fear or love? When has someone responded to you in fear or love?

8. Write a prayer to God about your fears. Meditate on Jesus' words from Matthew 6:25, 34: "Therefore I tell you, do not worry about your life, what you will eat or what you will drink, or about your body, what you will wear. . . . Do not worry about tomorrow, for tomorrow will bring worries of its own. Today's trouble is enough for today." How does this message resonate with you?

9. What did you learn from your grandparents or a mentor several generations older than you? What can you impart to the next generation?

10. Every day this week, write down a list of things for which you are grateful. Then write a prayer of thanksgiving to God. Observe how you feel after you do this.

Chapter 7

Courage

The Cyberbully

By now, it won't come as a shock to you that I am a minister who happens to be a woman. Sometimes I forget that this is controversial, a point of contention, or upsetting to people. I am simply following what I feel is God's call in my life. I am, however, frequently reminded of my uniqueness in a variety of ways, spanning from amusing to disturbing.

One of the most jolting experiences came during a conference called "Big Tent Christianity." This conference in Raleigh, North Carolina, was intended to bring together Christians of all denominations to discuss the future of the church and how we can work together toward the kingdom of God. I was on Twitter, providing snippets of sermons and conversations to followers so that people who couldn't attend might still engage. One person began to send me taunting messages. First, he asked how many conservatives were there. I responded that no poll was conducted but that I saw some conservative denominations represented. Then he messaged what he assumed was his ace in the hole, a quote from Paul: "Women should be silent in the church" (1 Cor 14:34).

This is a difficult passage, but it is hard to apply its message to all churches everywhere. Paul wrote specific letters to particular churches, celebrating their efforts or warning them that internal conflict would destroy them. In fact, women were deacons and church leaders. In his letter to the church at Philippi, Paul appeals to two women, Euodia and Syntyche, to agree together in the Lord and reminds them that they have "shared his struggles in the cause of the gospel" (Phil 4:3). They are among only a handful of people he mentions by name in his letter. Writing to the church of Rome, Paul commends Phoebe to the church as a "deacon in the church at Cenchreae. Give her, in the fellowship of the Lord, a welcome worthy of God's people, and support her in any business in which she may need your help, for she has herself been a good friend to many, including myself" (Rom 16:1-2). He goes on in that chapter to commend several other women. And let's not forget Lydia, who starts a house church after meeting Paul in Acts 16. So perhaps the Corinthian church had a specific group of women whom Paul believed were the source of conflict, or maybe he feared that, because they were so outspoken in a time when women had almost no power, they would further invite persecution and controversy. Other scholars believe that 1 Corinthians 14:34 was added later by someone other than Paul.

Regardless, this cyberbully was confronting me in the twenty-first century using a text that is no longer culturally relevant, much like the early church debate over whether or not to eat pork or keep kosher. More than that, he was trying to be mean. I chose not to respond; if he was trying to dehumanize me, it wasn't a conversation between two people who had mutual respect for each other. I went to bed troubled. What did everyone else who saw his comment think? I prayed that night for calm and for a solution.

When I returned to the conference the next morning, his comments were among the water-cooler chatter. The cyberbully was making jabs at anyone tweeting from the conference. He was bothered by the denominational unity that was evident in online conversations resulting from the speaker's statements. The cyberbully wanted to stay in his own silo. Paul, in 1 Corinthians 12:25-27 says, "There should be no division in the body, but that its parts should have equal concern for each other. If one part suffers, every part suffers with it; if one part is honored, every part rejoices with it. Now you are the body of Christ, and each one of you is a part of it." Throughout his letters, Paul is continually concerned about anything that is divisive. He wants to promote unity among the churches and keep them healthy. This isn't a proof text or a twisting of words like the cyberbully used; this is one of Paul's core messages. He's concerned about the survival of the church, just like those of us at the conference were. We wondered what the church will look like in the latter part of the twenty-first century. We pondered what issues to address and reconcile in order for the church to be faithful to Jesus' message of love and make it to the twenty-second century.

Those gathered at the Big Tent Christianity Conference continued to post messages online despite the cyberbully. Yes, his words were disturbing, but we were gathered as the body of Christ. Together, we represented a striving for wholeness in the kingdom of God that Jesus preached: "Where two or more are gathered in the name of God, I am there" (Matt 18:20). We weren't alone. We had the body of Christ and Jesus at the center.

Tornado Alley

The term "tornado alley" may be reserved for Midwestern states, but Kentucky has seen a large share of devastation from inclement weather, including tornadoes. Many Kentuckians consider ourselves part of the alley because of the frequency of tornado watches and warnings.

When I was about seven, I was riding in the middle of the bench seat of my parents' pickup truck between my mother and my sister, Jeri, on the way back to pick her up from school. It started sprinkling while my mom was driving on the interstate. I knew we were supposed to meet my dad at Hardee's for a milkshake in a few minutes, and he had probably already arrived from work.

Light rain turned into pounding rain and huge wind gusts in a matter of minutes. By the time my mother reached the exit after reducing her speed to a crawl, the sky was black, we could barely see a few feet in front of the truck, and the wind gusts pushed the truck back and forth. My mom stopped the truck on the ramp and wrapped an arm around me, and my sister did the same. They both wanted to protect me from the maelstrom outside. I vividly remember a stop sign spinning around and around, and I screamed when we all saw a dog clawing at the pavement before getting swept up in a gust.

"Don't look!" my mom cried out, forcing my head down. I looked intently at the designs on my shorts and cried while we were rocked from side to side and deafening wind and rain battered the truck. After a few minutes, the storm passed. As my mom drove slowly across the bridge to the restaurant, we saw the carnage. Roofs were torn off buildings. My dad's car was somehow spared when the restaurant sign had snapped not far away.

My mom and sister, though terrified, thought of the littlest one among them first. They wanted to keep me from being scared, and though I remember feeling helpless, I did feel better sitting between my mom and sister with their arms wrapped tightly around me. Their bravery kept me from outright panic and has taught me to remain calm during emergencies. After that experience, it takes a lot to make me scared of weather. Driving in rain and snow doesn't usually faze me although I know that I have a greater statistical likelihood of dying in that kind of bad weather than in a tornado.

When my niece Téa was about four, a tornado neared her daycare. The workers took all the children into the basement hallway and had them cover their heads. Her mother, my brave sister, Jeri, literally drove through the path of the storm to get to her child. She had to pull over multiple times because the wind and rain made it impossible to see, but she was determined to make it to my niece to calm her fears. When Jeri arrived at the daycare, Téa was calm.

"What did you do today?" Jeri asked.

"We had a tomato storm," Téa responded matter-of-factly.

"What's a tomato storm?" Jeri asked.

"It's where all the tomatoes from all around try to come and roll over us. But we hid so they didn't get us."

Jeri laughed, knowing that this misunderstanding caused a complete lack of fear in Téa, and she was excited not to have to answer endless questions about the weather after a day of driving through the worst of it. I laugh at the humor of the situation, but I also rest in the beauty of it. While Téa may never know what Jeri drove through to get to her that day, she has a million other reasons to know that her mother loves her.

The Panic before the Pulpit

Somewhere between amusing and anxiety-inducing was an experience in one Baptist church that shall remain unnamed. I was asked to preach one Sunday morning, which was a common request in my workplace. I was a bit nervous because I knew this church had some dysfunction. A minister confided in me before the service about particular issues related to the lack of church health and internal strife. About fifteen minutes before worship, I took my seat with my husband (also a minister) in the front pew.

People entering from the front of the sanctuary shook our hands. One gentleman shook my husband's hand first and then mine, and I heard a couple behind me say loudly, "Did you see that? He shook *his* hand first, but the preacher is the *lady!*" Next, a nervous teenage girl ran up to me and greeted me, saying that she would be introducing me and declaring that I was the first woman preacher they would have and that I would change everything. My eyebrows went up as I took her arm and said, "I'm just here to give the sermon today. I hope you all get something out of it, but we just need to get through today. Relax and just give a short introduction, and you'll be okay." The girl backtracked, "I didn't mean to make you nervous. It's just that everyone has been talking about this and has an opinion."

Great. So much for this being a regular Sunday.

The time came for me to give the sermon, and my knees felt like jelly as I walked toward the pulpit. I wondered what impact this would have on the church. It was hard to catch my breath, and I felt the grip of nausea in the pit of my stomach. It seemed that my mere presence as a woman was causing additional conflict. If they didn't like my sermon, would another woman be allowed in their pulpit in the next year? Or the next decade? I prayed on my way up, "Please God. This is in your hands. I'm just a person. I can't take on all these burdens, but you can. Help me."

I took a deep breath and preached a sermon focusing on the need for churches to go beyond their walls and to work alongside the community, building relationships. I asked, "What boundaries do we make for ourselves in our churches, our workplaces, our neighborhoods, and elsewhere that might keep others from hearing the good news of Jesus' love for all? . . . May we continually look for where God is working in the world, roll up our sleeves, and join in." I had to force myself not to choke on these words because I knew they were hard for the congregation to hear. Internal strife and conflict had led to more fighting than serving. What kind of witness were they to the community? Shouldn't we find ways to love one another and overcome disagreements over what the pastor looks like or what shirt or shoes he wears? (These were actual arguments that consumed that particular church.)

After the service, I was bombarded by a wide array of questions and comments. The first was jaw-dropping. A tall, older man shook my hand and said, "You looked so pretty up in that pulpit. If more women were like you, I could get used to a lady in the pulpit." I continued to shake his hand, speechless. What can anyone say to something that demeaning? I wondered if he'd heard a word I had said. Next, a man asked what I thought of a particular controversial author unrelated to my sermon. I deflected and asked what *he* thought about him, wanting to avoid conflict over such a minor issue. I went and comforted a group of people who were weeping as a man remembered his deceased wife. Finally, a woman told me that my sermon reminded her of an old friend who worked at AIDS Care Services and that she was inspired to volunteer there again.

At least I connected with one person, I thought.

Later, I reminded myself that I was preaching on Pentecost Sunday, when we remember how the Holy Spirit descended upon the apostles and the men and women gathered with them, and all of them spoke different languages and prophesied. What if the congregation drew a lot of different points out of my sermon that I had never considered? I do believe that, if our hearts are in the right place, God can be present in the process of speaking and listening beyond what we mean to convey. I asked for God's presence before the sermon because I could not do it alone. Who knows what the congregation heard when I opened my mouth?

That is the miracle of Pentecost. God was there even when I wasn't sure I wanted to be. I asked for God's help when I was terrified before I stepped into the fray. Courage isn't being fearless. It is showing up and doing what you feel is right despite the anxiety and fear that grip your earthly body. We can't do it alone. When I encounter something unsettling, I talk with family and friends whom I believe might have insights to share. Then, I take in their advice or comments and reflect on what that would look like in my life.

> *I have said this to you so that in me you may have peace. In the world you face persecution. But take courage; I have conquered the world. (John 16:33)*

After multiple experiences like the one I described, I listened to the advice of others with similar experiences and decided to see a counselor about the panic I felt before speaking in such situations. I highly recommend therapy. Counselors can help with anxiety, depression, marital conflict, and career discernment—and these are only a few of the issues that have brought dear friends to the therapist's chair. I shared with my counselor the "panic before the pulpit." Her response was something of a wonderful surprise.

First, she told me that no one can carry the weight of an entire gender or group when they enter into a situation. I needed to reframe these experiences. Instead, I should think of being a woman in the pulpit as a freeing experience. Male colleagues have a long tradition with which to connect—a certain way of dressing and speaking that has been laid out before them by tradition. The fact that I have no role model can be freeing. I am free to dress and speak how I choose. I did not grow up hearing a woman preacher, and neither did the people I preach to. I am a clean slate.

Second, she said that some amount of nervousness is always appropriate due to the nature of the job. This reminded me of a quote I had heard during Fred Craddock's sermon at the 2009 CBFNC General Assembly: "Nervousness is an indicator of the seriousness of the task at hand. If you are not nervous, you are doing it wrong." Comforting words from one of the best preachers in the United States.

Since that experience, I've preached multiple times. While I am still very nervous, I try to see my gender as freeing. I don't have to follow the same path as my male colleagues. I'm free to respond to the Spirit in this territory that still seems to be so uncharted by women.

Making Peace with Paul

Many people I know have a love/hate relationship with Paul. He made strong statements to particular communities during his ministry. Since then, those comments have been taken out of the context of those particular communities and touted like direct commandments to all people for all time. Otherwise, how can you mesh 1 Corinthians 14:33-35 with Galatians 3:28?

> As in all the churches of the saints, women should be silent in the churches. For they are not permitted to speak, but should be subordinate, as the law also says. If there is anything they desire to know, let them ask their husbands at home. For it is shameful for a woman to speak in church. (1 Cor 14:33-35)

> There is no longer Jew or Greek, there is no longer slave or free, there is no longer male and female; for all of you are one in Christ Jesus. (Gal 3:28)

These statements are at odds because Paul was speaking to two very different communities in two very different situations. His concern was not to create long-lasting doctrine but to put out fires in different churches. Paul thought that Jesus was coming back to earth quickly after his ascension, perhaps even before the end of Paul's life. If he had known we would still be quoting him two thousand years later, he might have edited his statements. This is especially true considering the fact that he respected and credentialed the female deacon Phoebe in his letter to the Romans (16:1). He also gives instruction about women serving as deacons in 1 Timothy 3:8-13. Paul clearly didn't have an issue with women in ministry, just with a particular group of women in the church at Corinth who were at the core of a specific conflict.

Yet his words have been twisted to suit a certain ideology. This ideology has been thrown in the faces of most women ministers, including myself, at some point before, during, or after ordination. So, while most people take issue with Paul, it's mostly about how his words have been twisted over time to exclude a portion of the population from fulfilling their calling from God (which I think trumps any words said by Paul, who was a human just like you and me).

A few years ago, still struggling with my feelings for Paul, I set out on a Mediterranean cruise with my in-laws. With stops in Rome, Crete, Sicily, Turkey, and Greece, it was one of the best gifts I could have received. Becky, Ryan's mother, expressed interest in seeing some of the religious sites along the way. Being total nerds for history and religion, Ryan and I enthusiastically agreed.

What I didn't bargain for was that I felt like I was tracking Paul's movements. In Turkey, our Muslim tour guide, John, spoke with great reverence about Paul. Talking about what a joy it was for Muslims to excavate the sacred ruins of Christians and help share their faith story, he led us to the heart of Ephesus. John told us the story of Paul preaching to the Ephesians in the 25,000-seat theater. He stated that the Ephesians probably made their living crafting and selling idols of the Roman gods. Paul's message to worship one God and put away idols caused a riot and led to his imprisonment a few hillsides over. Standing on the stage of the theater, I tried to imagine 25,000 people ready to riot and throw me into prison. Paul's courage, guts, and conviction were incredible.

In Athens, I retraced Paul's footsteps on the hill called the Areopagus (Mars Hill), rising above the agora, where noted speakers addressed the public. Paul preached to the Athenians, this time in a calm, respectful, interfaith dialogue, noting that they were wise because they even had a temple to an unknown God. Paul claimed to be there to discuss this unknown God. He was well received, and even though his ideas were not as popular there as in other locations, he was treated well and engaged in positive dialogue.

We ended the week in Rome, where both Peter and Paul bravely met their ends. There was no getting away from Paul. I had to face my feelings about his writings and separate the man and his words from how others had twisted them. Paul steadfastly met his audiences where they were, physically and mentally, and devoted his life to the church. It's not that he wasn't afraid, but that he was willing to risk everything for the Christ followers he had once killed before his conversion. He went from utter selfishness to a sacrificial life devoted to God and God's people. I have largely redeemed most of his writings for my own religious devotion and have come to admire aspects of his character. Mostly, I see him as a human being.

While able to accomplish extraordinary things, he experienced suffering and harbored anger.

Instead of holding on to any negative feelings about Paul, I choose to see him as a fascinating, complex person. It's far easier to engage someone once you humanize that person, living or dead. Granted, it's harder to get to know a deceased author, but you can learn about his character through his writing and try to relate to his circumstances. While I could resign myself to blame him for issues faced by women in ministry, it's far more productive to move forward, try to get to know him and understand his support for women in ministry, and separate him from the negative consequences of some of his words. It may be simpler for me to do this because, as a writer whose words can be taken out of context, I am especially sensitive to his situation. I'm grateful to have that in common with Paul and to have the chance to be forced to examine his works less critically. After all, we probably owe the existence of the church today to Paul for his courageous, tireless work. What lessons can we draw in the twenty-first century from Paul's daring spirit two millennia ago?

Reflection Questions

1. Write about some times when you felt afraid. What happened? Who or what threatened you?

2. Close your eyes and focus on those times. Jot down the emotions you had. Sit with those emotions for a moment. How do you feel about them?

3. How did you respond in these situations? Why do you think you responded in this way?

4. What Bible verses or stories remind you of your own life story? Why?

5. How can telling your own story be redemptive? What can you learn from that experience?

6. Where do you see God working in your times of fear? How can you rely on God more?

7. Think about the Scripture at the beginning of the chapter: "I have said this to you so that in me you may have peace. In

the world you face persecution. But take courage; I have conquered the world" (John 16:33). What does this mean for your life?

8. In this chapter, I stated, "Courage isn't being fearless. It is showing up and doing what you feel is right despite the anxiety and fear that grip your earthly body. We can't do it alone." In whom do you confide? Do you have a support network of people you can talk to? If not, think about the people with whom you can share life stories.

9. Which passages of the Bible do you find disturbing?

10. Have certain biblical passages or authors meant more to you at different stages of your life?

Conclusion

I hope that these stories have given you an idea of where God meets you in your life. I have found that God is absolutely everywhere. From the mundane to the humorous to the extraordinary, God is here with us. Most important, however, God is with us in the midst of grief and despair. In tragedies, God is in the response, not in the horrible act. God is in the volunteers after hurricanes, not in the disasters that break levees. No amount of bad theology can change that. Those who tell you that God is there to punish are probably dealing with their own lack of understanding or with guilt that they can't forgive.

I have met many people who have been hurt and broken by the church. It's a terrible thing that an institution meant to serve, love, and provide hope is the cause of so much pain. Many of us still want the church to be a place of refuge, and it is our responsibility to share our stories of healing for others who may have never seen this image of God projected through the church. I believe that only in sharing the honest, redemptive narratives of our lives may we relate to others and redeem our faith communities.

My passion for history tells me that there is much to retain and reuse in tradition. We can use some of the framework of the church from centuries past to provide a framework for the future. But we can only do this if we examine its redemptive qualities and its usefulness at reaching the painful places in the world, healing the wounds that people have suffered, and sustaining the community that gathers to worship and work in unity. There can no longer be a sense of clinging to the past merely for its own sake. We have to actively and tangibly want to examine our traditions, remake them if the situation calls for it, and use what works best to serve the children of God and their Creator.

I invite you to join with me in redeeming and reframing these Christian virtues through narrative. I invite you to email your stories to me (withusinthewilderness@gmail.com) so that I can share them on my blog, revlaurabarclay.blogspot.com, and we can join a greater community of Christians connecting through vulnerability. I want to hear your stories and see where God is working in your lives.

To share your story is to share a piece of yourself. I thank you for letting me share a lot of pieces of myself with you. I hope you connect with them. I hope they prompt you and empower you to do the same. Then, I hope you will be inspired to share them with me and with each other so that we can start a conversation. We will most likely learn that, although we are diverse in background and experience, the hopes and fears of the children of God are similar, and we are knitted together in this incredible journey of life by God's grace.

www.ingramcontent.com/pod-product-compliance
Lightning Source LLC
LaVergne TN
LVHW051745080426
835511LV00018B/3239